ORGANIZATIONAL ASSESSMENT:
DIAGNOSIS AND INTERVENTION

Rolf E. Rogers, Ph.D., CMC
Jane Y. Fong, Ph.D.

HRD Press
Amherst, Massachusetts

Copyright © 2000 by Rolf E. Rogers and Jane Y. Fong

All rights reserved. Any reproduction in any medium of the materials that appear in this book without written permission from HRD Press is a violation of copyright law.

Published by:

HRD Press
22 Amherst Road
Amherst, MA 01002
1-800-822-2801 (U.S. and Canada)
413-253-3488
413-253-3490 (FAX)
www.hrdpress.com

ISBN 0-87425-576-7

Cover design by Eileen Klockars
Editorial services by Suzanne Bay and Robie Grant
Production services by Clark T. Riley

Table of Contents

About the Authors v
Preface vii
Introduction to Organizational Assessment 1
- A Framework for Analysis 1
- How to Select Consultants for Organizational Assessment 3

Chapter   I.   Identifying Symptoms 11
Chapter   II.   Establishing the Facts 15
Chapter   III. Establishing Causes 23
- The Use of Questionnaires and Surveys 23
- How to Conduct Interviews and Analyze Interview Content 27
- The Use of Supervisor-Subordinate Data to Demonstrate Causation 35

Chapter   IV. Evaluating Alternatives 39
Chapter   V.   Selecting the Optimum Solution 45
Chapter   VI. Presenting Results 49
Chapter   VII. Other Considerations 53
Chapter   VIII. Case Studies 59
- Case Illustration: Susan Donnelley 61
- Case Study: The Selection 76
- Case Study: Chang *Versus* Collins 80
- Case Study: The Quality Engineering Group 85
- Case Study: Western Tire & Alignment 91

Appendices 103
References 119

About the Authors

Rolf E. Rogers, Ph.D., CMC, is a Certified Management Consultant and Professor Emeritus of Management at the California Polytechnic State University in San Luis Obispo, California. He has consulted internationally in the U.S., Canada, Australia, and Saudi Arabia. His clients include governments and private and public organizations. Dr. Rogers is the author of numerous published articles on management subjects. His books include *Organizational Theory* (Allyn & Bacon), *Corporate Strategy and Planning* (Grid/Wiley), *Organizational and Management Theory* (Wiley), and *Implementation of Total Quality Management* (Haworth). Dr. Rogers is the founder of Rogers and Associates, a management consulting firm that specializes in organizational assessment, strategic planning, quality management, team building, diversity management, conflict resolution, and executive coaching.

Jane Y. Fong, Ph.D. is a licensed Clinical Psychologist and Principal Consultant with Rogers and Associates. She has practiced clinical psychology for over 20 years, and incorporated management consulting in her career by working with family-owned businesses that experienced family-business role conflicts. Dr. Fong is a skilled psychotherapist, psychological diagnostician, personal/executive coach, and consultant. Her extensive understanding of human behavior enables her to assess many complex aspects of organizations, organizational behavior, and individual and group behavior in the workplace. She is also experienced in constructing survey instruments, analyzing data, and interpreting survey results. As an Asian-American, Dr. Fong's lifelong experience as a minority professional woman adds further depth to her diversity training. She is also a writer and editor for professional and lay publications.

PREFACE

Today's workplace is a far cry from that of 25 years ago. When Rolf Rogers began his career as a management professor, the class enrollment included only one or two females among 35 MBA students. Additionally, few ethnic minority students chose to enroll in business or management classes. Today, however, that same class is 50% female and more than 30% minority. In terms of class participation, students are more vocal, their questions are more direct and insightful, and they are more focused on how a particular issue affects them or applies to them as individuals.

These students are the workforce of tomorrow. Because modern organizations are changing at an ever-increasing pace, we can expect that change to be even be more intense when these same students enter the workforce. Clearly, traditional management styles, organizational structures, authority relationships, and methods of accomplishing work require adaptations to future changes, both known and unknown.

Rapid changes unquestionably indicate that Frederick Taylor's concepts of scientific management are no longer relevant and no longer workable. For example, his principles of authority and responsibility relationships were based on the notion of a relatively stable organization that experienced little or slow change over time. Taylor's ideas based on advances in "industrial engineering efficiency" are no longer applicable in twenty-first century America.[1]

Those days are gone. The rapid changes in technology, telecommunications, social values, and workforce composition render the "authoritarian" management style of the past obsolete. Attempts to deal with these cultural phenomena have resulted in many management "fads": Management by Objectives, Sensitivity Training, Project Management, Total Quality Management, Team Building, and so on.

---

[1] Frederick Taylor is often referred to as the "father of scientific management." His concepts and methods became the operating and management systems for American industry beginning in the late 1940s. See F. W. Taylor, *Scientific Management*. New York: Harper & Row, 1947.

One approach, Sensitivity Training, emerged as an organizational management application in the late 1960s and early 1970s. At that time, our culture was experiencing the painful realities of the Civil Rights movement, the Women's Movement, our involvement in the political-military struggles in Southeast Asia, and other national crises. The Equal Employment Opportunity Commission was created in the late 1960s to address discrimination against minorities and women in hiring, inequality of salaries, problems with promotion, and other such issues. Leaders in workplace management were forced to develop new approaches to respond to cultural processes that disrupted the nation itself.

Sensitivity Training assumed that if managers got to know themselves, their peers, and their subordinates better, they would then become more effective managers. Executives and managers were sent to "retreats" away from the home office to a "neutral" or "calming" environment where they would benefit from their "introspection" and self-analysis. Training sessions were conducted by "facilitators" who offered "human relations" exercises that involved "dyads," "triads," "group-on-group observation," and other interactional role-playing methods. Without necessarily discussing the participants' inner selves or personal drives, these methods were assumed to enable managers to become "better" or "more sensitive" persons, or "more sensitive" to the needs of peers and subordinates.

After the weekend retreat, the manager returned to work Monday morning ready to try the new "sensitive" approach to management. How did this work? Employees were confronted with their manager's unexpected, new, and unpredictable behavior. Not knowing why the manager exhibited these new, different, and surprising behaviors, employees became very anxious and confused. They asked themselves and each other: "What's wrong with the boss? How should I react to him or her? What does all this mean? Why is he or she doing this?" Needless to say, if a manager's behavior changes and the employees have not received information on why or how, their reactions naturally will contain varying amounts of anxiety, confusion, and **worry.** Faced with confused, anxious, or even negative reactions from employees, the "sensitive" manager quickly abandons his or her newly learned behaviors, and resumes the previous "normal" behaviors that employees had become accustomed to.

Since these approaches were theoretically sound and not "wrong," why did they fail, or why did they not work the way they were intended to? There are two basic reasons:

- **Failure to institute total system implementation.** All of these approaches are based on "total application." They were designed to be implemented as a total system and applied on a sustaining basis so that Step 1 was followed by Step 2, then Step 3. We found in our consulting engagements that few, if any, of these "systems" or concepts were implemented in total as they were designed to be. Companies in almost all cases would pick and choose the aspects they liked and would implement those steps selectively. Because these systems were designed with sequential steps and as total applications, companies that chose to use only parts of and not the entire system noted the system's failure, became disenchanted, and discontinued using it.

- **Lack of continuous positive reinforcement.** The second reason is not as obvious as the first, but is significantly more important. All of these approaches were based on the assumption of "continuous positive reinforcement." When managers' behaviors were changed in order to better manage employees (as in the above Sensitivity Training example), employees were not all able to adapt to abrupt behavioral changes. Anyone working with people on a daily basis knows that if behavior is not reinforced (either positively or negatively), that behavior will fade over time. This "Skinnerian fading effect" was first used by the late B. F. Skinner to describe the results of his numerous operant conditioning experiments.[2]

Thus, considering these two processes, any or all of the above-mentioned management fads would not or did not last in organizations that did not implement them in full, did not prepare employees for the behavioral changes managers exhibited, and did not also include employees in making behavioral changes. In short, training for change, applications of new management tools, or major systems change must include all persons at all levels of an organization.

We recognize that problems in organizations will exist as long as there are organizations. An organization, like a family, will encounter problems from time to time depending on the stage of its development, the personalities of its members, the methods that the group uses to cope with

---

[2]B. F. Skinner developed the relationship of stimulus, response, and reinforcement in shaping behavior. Relevant to this discussion, Skinner consistently found that behavior that is not reinforced will extinguish (e.g., "fade out") over time. See B.F. Skinner, *Contingencies of Reinforcement* (New York: Appleton-Century-Crofts, 1969).

crises or change, and the quality and maintenance of team efforts. Successfully negotiating through problems and resolving problems distinguishes the growing, healthy organization (or family) from those that remain stagnant and fraught with internal problems, suffer from low productivity and efficiency, and undergo many other organizational pains. The framework we offer here involves evaluation, diagnosis, intervention, and periodic follow-up on how the organization functions. This problem-solving approach can be applied to organizations regardless of changes in technology or people.

Rolf E. Rogers, Ph.D., CMC
Jane Y. Fong, Ph.D.

Introduction to Organizational Assessment
A Framework for Analysis

Someone once suggested that all problems in an organization are management problems. Broadly speaking, this is probably true. Management, after all, is legally responsible, one way or another, for almost everything that happens in an organization. Management has the authority to change the process under which organizations operate.

From strategy formulation to change implementation, management decides what will be done, how it will be done, who will do it, and what the ultimate outcome should be. Unfortunately, this is seldom a precise or highly predictable process. Every day, organizations fail because they selected the wrong strategy, the wrong people, the wrong market, the wrong equipment, the wrong product or service, or the wrong process. Unlike the natural sciences, the uncertainty and risk of choosing one strategic or operational alternative over another can be the difference between success and failure in any organization.

Can we achieve certainty in this decision-making process? Probably not. However, we *can reduce the degree of uncertainty*: We can develop and follow a consistent framework for analyzing the organizational processes in order to make the best decisions.

In this book, we use a time-tested practical framework for identifying and analyzing organizational issues in a consistent manner. This step-by-step approach is *not* a theory or set of hypotheses, but a framework that has been used by organizational consultants for some time. The approach consists of five phases that are performed in sequence. Each step builds on the completion of the former one:

1. Identify symptoms (symptoms).
2. Establish the facts (fact finding).
3. Establish causes (causation).

4. Evaluate alternative approaches to addressing the problems (alternatives analysis).
5. Select and justify the best solution (optimization).

Our purpose in writing this book is to provide a practical guide for identifying and assessing organizational problems and for choosing optimum solutions. We intentionally bypass academic discussions of underlying theories of management — many books already exist on the subject. In this book, we describe each step and demonstrate it through the use of the case of Susan Donnelley. Other cases are presented to provide readers with supplemental organizational situations for further personal study.

Using the illustration below, readers can familiarize themselves with the Five Steps and our methods of case analysis.

The Five-Step Framework

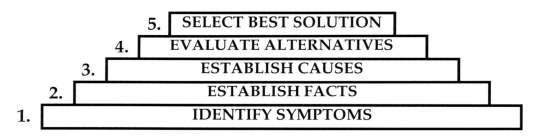

How to Select Consultants for Organizational Assessment

In this section, we offer our experience and thoughts on types of organizational problems or changes that require the use of particular categories of consultants. First, the "easier" projects to address involve *technical* issues that have practical and clearer implications for organizations than issues that involve *individuals and groups of people* within the organization. Technical needs or problems within an organization do not involve "people" as primarily factors or the focus of concern. These can be viewed as "process" or "company maintenance" problems, which include but are not necessarily limited to: problems with equipment or dilemmas with facilities or space, improving or changing production processes, implementing a new quality control system, redesigning a product, updating management information systems, addressing any legal problems, and evaluating financial issues.

Because these "problems" require specific types of expertise *and* intimate knowledge of the organization so affected, the use of internal consultants (or the use of upper-level managers themselves) can result in the most cost-effective approach *and* ensure the desired outcome for the organization. In certain types of these cases, management might choose to outsource or subcontract for a specialized service. For example, a counseling firm is retained to provide services for an employee assistance program or a security firm is employed to improve physical security systems and provide security officers. Most organizations handle these technical dilemmas with a great deal of confidence and competence; thus, we do not dwell further on this topic.

Now, on to the more complex topic: When management has decided that the company needs an organizational assessment and analysis or organizational change or development, and its complicated technical problems require consulting, how can the organization make wise and judicious decisions? What type of consultant should the organization hire to meet its needs? If the desired consulting expertise is available from persons within the organization, what are the advantages and disadvantages of using an internal consultant? What are the advantages and disadvantages of hiring an independent external consultant? How much is the project going to cost? Once an organization has decided to work with a consultant, upper management confronts these and many other practical questions too numerous to list here.

Regrettably, the organizational landscape is littered with the ruins of the results of using the "wrong" consultant. The first major decision that determines success or failure of an organizational assessment is the option to use an "external" (independent) consultant or an "internal" (organizational employee) consultant. To assist decision-makers in thinking through this process, we offer important guidelines that enable both management and consultants to make informed decisions.

Generalist vs. Specialist Expertise. By definition, a "generalist" is an individual who has the training, experience, and expertise to look carefully at the client organization against the background of prevailing market trends and economic factors. The generalist consultant can be a referral from another organization who has worked with him or her, or through industry-wide reputation. His or her vita must demonstrate relevant knowledge areas and skills. At a minimum, the generalist:

1. Knows how the client company performs within that industry.
2. Has a comprehensive knowledge of how industry in general, and the client's industry in particular, functions.
3. Is familiar with the client's industry from a strategic point of view.
4. Knows organizational structure and design in that industry, and what works or doesn't work.
5. Knows different management practices, compensation systems, profit margins, sales ratios, and international trends.
6. Is personable and relates well to both management and subordinates.
7. Demonstrates ethical professional practices.
8. Has access to other consultants and/or resources, should there be a need to subcontract services.
9. Can guarantee completion of the project in phases and timelines with presentable products to management.

These characteristics represent only a sample set of skills, knowledge, and style that management ought to consider when hiring a consultant. As mentioned below, one organization's assessment had to be done over again because management chose someone who was not well received by the organization.

"Specialists" are those persons with in-depth expertise in a specific area of consulting. These may include industrial/organizational psychologists, financial experts (e.g., CPAs), management information systems consultants, or employment or business attorneys. In addition to demonstrating specific skills and knowledge, the specialist, like the generalist, must be ethical, reliable, able to work with others (in this case, management), and be able to "deliver" the required services or products.

Generalists and specialists often work collaboratively: Many generalist consultants bring in specialists as "subcontractors" to address specific issues. In the Susan Donnelley case (detailed elsewhere in this book), we brought in a clinical psychologist consultant to work individually with Ms. Donnelley on issues of personal stress and her behavior with her subordinates, coaching her on alternative ways of working with employees, etc. In other engagements, we brought in other relevant specialists. For example, a CPA was hired to examine the financial system in one company; an industrial engineer was subcontracted to evaluate a company's production system; an attorney was hired to evaluate the client's contracts and protection from product liability.

In these situations, the generalist consultant is retained for the engagement in its entirety; he or she maintains primary responsibility and oversight for the project, and integrates and coordinates the total assessment effort. This total project management offers significant advantage and cost savings for the client company: Obviously, when a "project manager" is in charge of the assessment, the organization's managers do not have to identify, find, and hire the necessary specialists and do not have to coordinate, integrate, and otherwise make practical sense of the individual and separate findings that specialists submit to them.

Cost/benefit analysis. When management confronts organizational problems, executive ask themselves questions such as: "What will happen if the decline in sales is not reversed? What will happen if the employee turnover rate in the engineering department continues to increase? How long can we afford to lose contracts? What will happen if employee morale continues to decline?" Regrettably, financial estimates on such conditions cannot always be answered, so accurate dollar costs are extremely difficult to determine.

On the matter of costs in hiring consultants to investigate company problems, special care must be used in conducting a cost/benefit analysis, which typically involves "number crunching." Management must ask itself: What is the dollar cost of using an external versus an internal consultant? The problem, of course, is more complex than financial costs: "What is the ultimate cost of not having our problem reviewed or resolved?" This second set of numbers is usually very difficult to estimate.

External vs. Internal Consultants. When considering using an external or internal consultant, management might wonder, "What, exactly, are the qualifications of the external compared to those of the internal consultant (if one is available)?" In many cases, the education, experience, and knowledge of both the internal and external consultants are comparable (and perhaps even competitive in the marketplace!). Because the organizational assessment includes employee response to surveys and/or interviews, answers to the following questions may be the most decisive determinant: "How well can this consultant relate to my employees? How well will employees cooperate and relate to this consultant? Are there any characteristics or features about this consultant that would 'turn off' employees?" In other words, management looks carefully at the "social" presentation of the consultant so that the consultant's initial contact with employees is neutral (at the very least) or positive (the most desired effect). The goal is to ensure rapport between the consultant and employees as quickly as possible.

Organizational Resources: Using Internal Consultants. In this phase, management needs to ask itself "Now that we have defined the problems, do we have expertise and capability within our organization to perform the required assessment? Do we have talent to identify problems in greater detail and to pose solutions to the problems?" Small companies typically do not have this capability, and are forced to retain outside expertise to help address the organization's problem(s). In large companies, an internal consultant with expertise in financial planning, accounting, statistical measures, or forecasting can be used to great advantage in examining the number-crunching estimates of cost/benefit analysis mentioned above.

Disadvantages of using internal consultants. If an efficacious organizational assessment is to be conducted, and if the company is genuinely invested in obtaining important facts surrounding problems, management must be able to answer this question: "Can the internal consultant successfully identify symptoms or establish useful facts with the current composition of employees in the troubled unit or department?" If this question cannot be readily answered, internal consultants will likely produce inadequate or irrelevant results. Sadly, internal consultants' efforts can even be "sabotaged" (intentionally or unintentionally) by the organization's employees, as indicated by the case example that follows.

In one of our consulting engagements, the organization had used internal consultants to conduct employee surveys and interviews as preparation for a major reorganization. The results of these efforts did not make sense to the chief executive officer: Employee response patterns were distorted; underlying realistic problems were not adequately identified; and findings were rather "bland." Disappointed with the assessment and still troubled by the organization's internal problems, the CEO retained our services to repeat the assessment using our methodology. During the phase in our project when we interviewed employees, we discovered that many employees did not trust the internal consultants; employees felt that the consultants were biased, or that whatever employees told the internal consultants would be passed on directly to their supervisors! The employees' perceptions, anxieties, and worries clearly influenced the poor outcomes of the assessment conducted by the company's own experts.

Further, other consequences of this first choice became painfully evident to the CEO: "wasted" time and effort on the part of the internal consultant; costs in the form of salary/wages paid to the consultant for his or her "expertise" and time taken to perform the assessment were not recoverable; the consultant's reputation as an untrustworthy individual was inadvertently reinforced in the course of this project; some employees selected to participate in that assessment experienced temporary workplace anxiety or annoyance; and finally, there were many lost person-hours of employee work time.

Considerations in Using External Consultants. Upper management might ask, "If both external and internal consultants have similar expertise and backgrounds, how competently can an outside consultant deal with the organization's problems or issues, compared to our inside consultant?" In asking this question, the managers are likely concerned that the outsider does not know very much about the organization, would have to spend large amounts of time in early phases of the contract to "research," "do homework," or otherwise become familiar with the dynamics and players within the organization.

While we respect this concern, we remind managers that the experienced external consultant has worked with many other organizations with similar problems. He or she might have an insight into organizational consequences of various alternative solutions that the internal consultant does not have (i.e., downsizing, re-engineering, plant closures, and others). Further, the external consultant enjoys a wide latitude of independence that the internal consultant might not have. Additionally, the consultant's professional reputation impacts immensely on employee cooperation and response: If employees have some knowledge or acquaintance with the consultant, and if employees consider the consultant objective, personable, trustworthy, patient, and nonthreatening to them personally, such employee reaction to the consultant is a major advantage (and therefore carries weight) in management's decision to hire or not hire certain consultants.

Management consultants typically deal with organizational matters that involve people and not machines, technical systems, or other nonhuman applications. As such, relationships are formed between the consultant and workers. In our consulting methodology, we use interviewing to obtain qualitative and revealing information about organizational and interpersonal dynamics. In the course of interviews, we have found that many employees speak more "freely" to an outsider and openly share information that they would not disclose to an insider. This process is similar to counseling, in which the client readily confides in the therapist and knows that the therapist does not live with the client in daily life, and would not divulge confidential information, or otherwise adversely affect the client.

Other considerations: project timelines. How much time is available to identify and resolve a problem? If there are time constraints, how do these affect the consultation? For external consultants, timelines are typically agreed on in the contracting phase. Additional resources can be obtained by the consultant to meet requirements imposed by time constraints. For internal consultants, they might not have these options: Due to their employee status, they are subject to organizational strictures such as previous commitments or other projects or intra-organizational transfers, sick leave, or compensation issues.

Consultant selection strategy. Clearly, the decision of whether to use external or internal consultants can be a complex one. Because particular types of organizations and industries have unique requirements and practices, it is extremely difficult to make general recommendations on types of consultants needed. To assist managers in thinking through the process, we present the following sample strategy:

Identify the problem: Employee turnover continues to increase in the engineering department.

- **Decide on whether or not to conduct an organizational assessment**, if the management agrees an assessment is needed;

- **Decide whether to use an internal consultant (especially for technical or "housekeeping" problems) or an external consultant**.
Refer to Table 1: Consultant Decision-Making Factors.

Table 1: Consultant Decision-Making Factors

	Factors to Consider	Priority/or Importance	
		Manager 1 Manager 2 etc.	Manager average
1.	Cost: How much money do we have to spend on this project?		5
2.	Cost: How much will this project cost?		9
3.	Generalist required?		8
4.	Specialist required?		9
5.	Expertise/experience?		9
6.	Employee bias or negative attitude about internal consultant?		10
7.	Time: How quickly must this be done?		10
8.	Is it a people problem?		10
9.	Is it a technical problem?		2
10.	Other factor?		
11.	Other factor?		
12.	Other factor?		

Note: These factors are not arranged in any particular sequence.

Instructions: To estimate priorities, indicate how important each factor is in hiring a consultant by rating each factor on the scale (ranging from 1 to 10), indicating:

1= (low) not important; 5= moderately important; 10= most important (high)

Example problem. Conduct an organizational assessment to determine why employee turnover continues to increase in the engineering department.

External vs. internal consultant: As illustrated in the table above, the three major priorities are (1) employee bias, (2) time, and (3) people problems. In this case, the choice would be to retain an outside consultant since he or she would meet these requirements more effectively than an internal consultant.

This table can be used to prioritize different variables. The factors above are not listed in any particular sequence. The table can be modified by adding or by omitting items to suit the needs of the organization. We suggest that several managers (if applicable) estimate the value of each factor associated with the organizational problem, first individually and later as a group by calculating the average score or mean for each factor.

In summary, it is apparent that the decision of whether to use an internal or external consultant is a complex one. Because particular types of organizations and industries have unique requirements and practices, it is difficult to generalize. However, the approach suggested above should be helpful in assisting management in this decision.

Chapter I
Identifying Symptoms

Facts and symptoms are often identified simultaneously and often used interchangeably. We agree that facts can be symptoms, just as symptoms can be facts. However, each should be viewed as distinctly different from the other and should be addressed separately in any consultation engagement.

By definition, symptoms are *manifestations, signs, or indications of underlying problems*. When one has a cough, for example, the cough can be one sign of any number of problems — including the common cold, an allergy, or something stuck in one's throat. *Symptoms might or might not truly explain what is really going on beneath the surface.* For example, an interesting (and sometimes confusing) symptom that can occur in any organization is employee turnover:

> In one of our engagements, management had identified low compensation to explain high turnover in the company's engineering department.[1] During our fact-finding phase, we obtained factual data to assess whether the rate of employee exodus was low, average, or high. The company's turnover data (i.e., facts) indicated above-average numbers of employees leaving the company in a given time period, compared to industry rates and to the company's turnover history during the same period in prior years.
>
> When we looked at wages and benefits, we discovered that the engineers' salaries were not only competitive, but were actually above the average in that geographical area! In this case, compensation was clearly not the actual cause of the turnover problem.

What are the symptoms in this case? Obviously, the symptom was employee attrition. What are the facts? By definition, facts are *tangible and actual events or objects that exist in reality.* In the above example, the facts included (1) high turnover rates, (2) competitive salaries, and (3) management's serious concern, "What's going on here?" As consultants, our task was to uncover or discover the reasons why turnover existed at this alarming rate.

---

[1] Employee turnover is a symptom, of course, for which compensation might not be the cause!

Special Symptoms: Distortions Due to Perceptions

Interpersonal perception has long been discussed in formal psychological research. We define perception as *the application of one's own values and standards of behavior to another person*. Here, we emphasize that *issues involving people are almost always based on perception*. Because perceptions are not tangible objects, perceptions can be readily influenced, especially when the perceiver depends on the ideas or judgment of others whose opinion he or she holds in high regard.

In attempts to "objectify" perceptions or to eliminate perceptual distortions, various methods are used to verify or to counter specific perceptions: Our judicial system uses the "reasonable person" concept; anthropologists use "value-free analysis"; psychologists apply "reality testing." These processes remove, separate out, or minimize our own standards or values to sort through distortions in our perception of others.

Unfortunately, rational thinking or reality testing is often considered irrelevant in addressing human behavior in the workplace. In group settings (including workplaces), the prevailing attitude often overrides the perceptions of any lone employee. Most organizations have a unique workplace culture and value system. Members' expectations are based on the organization's traditions, practices, and customs. In that organizational culture, human behavior becomes predictable over time: When a group offers the same or similar perceptions, these perceptions are much more difficult to ignore and often difficult to counteract. A group's perception of any manager, especially if congruent among the group members, is a tough nut to crack!

Typically, managers are viewed as "role models," and their behavior is subjected to more scrutiny than that of a peer or colleague. Here, we can best illustrate how interpersonal perception works by using the case of Susan Donnelley:

> Susan had been selected as the new manager of the legal department of Star Corporation.[1] One year into her new position, management was bombarded by employees in the legal department and complaints from its clients about Susan's leadership and management style. Susan was reported as "autocratic," "a micro-manager," "rude," "untrustworthy," "unreliable," and a "lousy manager."

---

[1]See *The Selection* in Chapter VIII, Case Studies.

Identifying Symptoms

What were the symptoms in this case? When people complained about Susan or described her negative behavior, managers above Susan were persuaded that if several employees made similar complaints, then,

- "People are unhappy with her; therefore, Susan is a problem."
- "The department's performance is suffering — and it is because of her."
- "We made a mistake in appointing her to this position."

This type of thinking affects interpersonal relationships, expectations, motivation, and individual employee performance and group performance as a whole. As upper management arrived at these conclusions, their conclusions also become symptoms!

Major difficulties arise if symptoms are not identified separately from the facts surrounding the symptoms. In the example above, if corrective action is taken on the symptom alone, the actual underlying cause is not being addressed adequately. The original symptom might be "fixed," but other symptoms might eventually emerge — other signs, other indications of unsolved or unresolved problems.

By the same token, if Susan were terminated from her position as manager, the symptoms (i.e., complaints about her managerial abilities) would be removed, but important underlying causes would still exist. Further investigation must be conducted in order to uncover the real organizational problems that contributed to these symptoms. The next step, fact finding, can prove informative and productive toward this objective.

Chapter II
Establishing the Facts

Fact finding can be a cumbersome, sometimes monotonous process, but it is a necessary one. Depending on the initial perception of the problem, the organizational climate, management resources, internal structure for addressing problems, and other factors, fact finding can be a long detailed endeavor or a short review. It might include evaluations of financial performance, sales, production, quality, personnel, and other data. It might include industry comparisons and ratios, regional statistics, labor markets, competitive performance, or simply the verification of an easily identifiable issue.

We illustrate our fact-finding process by using an analogy of a first meeting between a doctor and a new patient: When Mr. Jones arrives at Dr. Stevens' office, the patient has already formed an opinion on what might be wrong. Dr. Stevens listens carefully to Mr. Jones' description of problems or symptoms. At the same time, Dr. Stevens keeps in mind that his immediate task is to arrive at a medical diagnosis based on *facts* of the patient's medical history.

To do this, he examines Mr. Jones with a health *systems review* and a probing interview on the patient's past history, and *evaluates his current status* by using proven medical and scientific methods (he takes blood pressure, listens to the heart and lungs, etc.). By the end of the office visit, Dr. Stevens renders a tentative diagnosis, pending results of laboratory tests, X-rays, or other diagnostic procedures. As a responsible physician, Dr. Stevens recommends treatment only when all medical facts and assessments are available.

In much the same way, we arrive at a baseline understanding of the *organizational facts* and the *organization's current problems* by performing an initial review of the organization. In the first consultation meeting, the client executives typically describe the troublesome situation and discuss what *they* think lies behind the problems. Too often managers *assume* they know what the underlying causes are. *More often than not, they have not defined the facts or they are addressing symptoms only.*

What, then, is the bottom line here? At this phase, the consultant is differentiating organizational symptoms from possible facts. Just as Dr. Stevens does not recommend specific treatment to his patients until all medical evidence is in, *organizational consultants cannot (should not) identify underlying issues or problems until they have clear answers to the question "What is really going on?"*.

In order to establish facts relevant to the organization's problems, we first examine the organization's systems to determine what is contributing to its current difficulties. Using the medical model described above, we examine the organization's history, systems, and current functioning. To assess conditions that might be contributing to the client's stated organizational problems, we obtain information by reviewing all organizational systems:

1. Strategy Formulation, Development, and Planning (the organization's mission, goals, objectives).
2. Operational Planning (budgets, unit plans).
3. Financial Performance (ROI, profit contribution).
4. Product/Service Costs (pricing, accuracy, reality test).
5. Sales Performance (international, regional, production, service).
6. Work Process (technology, equipment).
7. Quality Management/Performance (standards, measurement).
8. Human Resource Management (policies, benefits, civil rights).
9. Measurement Systems (feedback, time, accuracy, variation).
10. Corrective Action System (feedback, reaction time, change management).

A thorough analysis of these organizational systems leads to an informed position for the consultant: We are now able to *pinpoint obvious problems* and to *evaluate management's initial perceptions* about what they think the problems are. For example, the previous chapter discussed a turnover problem through identifying symptoms and establishing facts.

Special Topics in Fact Finding: Masked Facts in the Selection of Managers

In many organizations, most of these ten systems are already in place. We refer the reader to numerous books, reference materials, and video and audio materials, readily available, that describe these organizational structures. For our purposes, we wish to highlight special topics related to manager issues which are often overlooked and which contribute in powerful ways to serious (and in some instances, legal) problems for the organization.

In the fact-finding step and occasionally in the establishing-causes phase, we examine unacknowledged organizational dynamics, which are often directly linked to "people problems" such as a manager's difficulties in leadership, in communications, or in daily interaction. In some organizations, these difficulties are readily apparent. Other organizations can act as if these problems do not exist. More than likely, underlying daily persistent organizational practices and managerial behavior exist but remain unarticulated or unacknowledged.

These unstated dynamics comprise what we call "masked facts" and are destructive forces that erode the organization from within. Relevant to our discussion in this book, we begin by looking at masked facts related to Susan Donnelley's appointment as the new manager of her department by asking at least three important questions and attempting to pinpoint explanations for the problems in her department:

1. How was the individual (i.e., Susan) selected for that management position?
2. What specialized training opportunities were offered to or required of her?
3. How well does she "match" the organizational culture and the subordinates in the department?

Employee Selection. Several considerations must be kept in mind when examining employee hiring, especially how managers are hired. First, there are no standard rules organizations must follow when hiring managers. One organization's advertising and review of applications can differ substantially from that of others. A common practice that raises ethical and/or legal questions is to advertise widely in industry publications, even though a particular individual with specific characteristics has already been implicitly selected:

In the case we refer to as *The Selection*, cited in this book, a woman (Susan Donnelley) from outside the company was selected as the new manager of a department. A longtime employee in the company (the interim manager) was a finalist for the position. He had looked forward to a confirmed, official managerial position and alluded to that with his peers and superiors. No one hinted for him to anticipate otherwise. When he learned that a woman was chosen over him as manager, he sued the company on the basis of discrimination due to gender, age, and race.

By selecting Susan over other candidates, upper management was obviously interested in hiring a woman manager. Yet no advertising stated "Women and minorities are encouraged to apply." One wonders how many applications from qualified men were (or were not) reviewed!

In other organizations, numerous applications might be received. One individual is selected for the position. After a reasonable time period has passed, candidates not chosen are notified. "Thank you for your interest in our organization. Your credentials are impressive. However, we have hired an individual whom we feel best suits our needs." For persons actively hunting for work, receiving such a rejection letter raises questions of how honest the organization was in its advertising and in its subsequent communication (if any) by follow-up phone calls or letters to applicants.

A second consideration involves the screening process: The selection of individuals for managerial positions is typically based on the person's "track record" or career resume, reference letters, educational status, in-depth interviews, and a period of probation on the job.[1] While these sources of information are important and extremely useful, there is an additional cost-effective and reliable method many organizations do not use: *Individual psychological assessment and testing*.

When used in personnel selection, psychological assessment information adds important dimensions to employee selection and serves a preventative purpose. Testing can describe leadership abilities, assess for psychological strengths and weaknesses, identify personality disturbances or mental stresses that adversely impact on work or interpersonal functioning, and identify temporary or transient problems such as situationally produced depression or anxiety (which affect 90% of the general population at one time or another in life).

Numerous published psychological tests are available and cover areas such as aptitude, psychomotor, job knowledge, vocational interest, and personality assessment.[2] Psychological personnel testing is most useful, valid, and reliable when conducted and interpreted by a licensed psychologist with an expertise in diagnostic evaluation or personnel selection.

---

[1] Bear in mind, however, our admonition that many organizations assume, falsely so, that technical expertise in a given area and quality leadership skills are synonymous.
[2] See L. L. Byars and L. W. Rue (1997). *Human Resource Management* (5th Ed). New York: McGraw Hill.

Unfortunately for our client, The Star Corporation, the selection of Susan Donnelley as department manager did not include personnel or psychological testing. Later on in our consultation, we recommended to upper management that psychological counseling would adjust some of the manager's inappropriate behaviors and enhance her leadership capacities.[1]

Affirmative Action. Another masked problem area involves the role of affirmative action policies, especially in federal agencies or in organizations that receive substantial funding from governmental sources. We do not take a position here for or against affirmative action. Our purpose here is to alert readers to complex problems that can come up when one candidate is chosen over another, especially when a qualified individual has already spent most of his or her work life with the client organization.

The Susan Donnelley case reflected an attempt by upper management to add a woman manager to its roster. Yet the company did not anticipate that its loyal employee, the interim manager, would take legal action because he was not selected. This organization was thus caught in a significant dilemma: Damned if you exercise affirmative action; damned if you don't!

Specialized Training. A third possible masked fact involves special training opportunities and supervision for managers: Does the organization in fact offer or support training? Numerous training programs are available and are offered through one's company or through educational institutions or private training companies. They might include one-day seminars to week-long ones covering topics such as leadership skills, conflict resolution, motivating employees, corporate games playing, and stress management. It is beyond the scope of this book to describe training opportunities in detail.

We draw your attention, however, to two crucial areas that all organizations must address today in their daily functioning: *Sexual harassment* and *competence in diversity*. These areas have taken on profound economic implications for any organization found "guilty" of sexual/racial harassment or noticeably different treatment of women, minorities, the handicapped, gays/lesbians, or aging workers.

Sexual Harassment. A relatively new phenomenon in the American workplace, sexual harassment legal statutes have been constructed, implemented, and applied only in recent decades. If and when sexual harassment occurs, many workers do not know about actions they can take within their organization.

---

[1] See the cases of Susan Donnelley and The Selection in Chapter VIII, Case Studies.

In one of our engagements, for example, an employee being interviewed in the course of the organizational assessment revealed the high distress she was experiencing due to sexual harassment from a superior. This woman did not know what to do and was on the verge of filing a lawsuit against the company. In discussion with her, we urged her to take appropriate steps by first speaking with the company's human resource specialist. We also obtained the employee's permission to speak with her superiors about the problem. Senior management was not aware of the situation until it was brought to its attention by the consultant.

The professional literature and popular media have covered this topic on a regular, if not a daily, basis. We refer the reader to readily available material rather than describe it in any detail in this book. However, we urge consultants to review the extent to which a client organization has implemented prevention training or posted worker rights regarding sexual harassment in the workplace.[1]

Diversity Competence. In today's cultural climate, managers must be knowledgeable about behaviors, treatment, or policies related to persons who are "culturally different" and to function effectively in the midst of these differences. Specific training (and reinforcement) in this knowledge, often referred to as "diversity competence," must thus be an essential part of any managerial position. The following example highlights a unique but increasingly present worker composition in many organizations:

> In the QEG[2] case, the work group consisted of Vietnamese, Hindu, Pakistani, Hispanic, Caucasian, and African-American men and women employees. Persons from different ethnic/cultural backgrounds were "thrown together" and most lacked cross-cultural understanding about each other. A male Caucasian manager who had little understanding of his subordinates' languages, culture, or behavioral differences supervised the department. Many misunderstandings occurred. Departmental performance suffered dramatically. Multiple problems occurred in the department. The manager, rightly so, felt nearly devoid of personal control in the department.

This work group might seem unusual, but its multicultural composition offered a unique opportunity for training and team building. Over a period of several weeks, we made use of the racial/ethnic/cultural/behavioral diversity readily apparent in the daily life of this group in two-hour group

---

[1] See Appendix 1. Sexual Harassment Policy Statement, California Dept. of Employment and Fair Housing. See Appendix 2. Sexual Harassment Prevention Checklist.
[2] For a description of this group, see the QEG case in Chapter VIII.

sessions. We specifically focused on language communications (native versus American English), social difficulties or confusion raised when subgroups spoke in their native tongues, and misunderstandings that had already occurred in the group.

We also looked at nonverbal behaviors that mean one thing in a particular culture, but mean something else in another culture. We examined employees' use of time, values, standards, relationship to peers and to authority, and other culture-bound characteristics that impacted on employee functioning at work.

In a relatively short time period, many misconceptions and misunderstandings were clarified among all workers in the department. These workers came to appreciate and understand co-workers from different native origins. Further, they better understood their supervisor's management methods and his style of interpersonal relating. In turn, the manager learned how to mobilize cooperation among his diverse employees.

Manager- Employee/Climate Match. Here, we look at traditional types of daily managerial functioning — autocratic, democratic, laissez-faire, etc. All of these managerial characteristics can be productive, if the subordinates within the department function according to the manager's style. In other words, if a laissez-faire manager is placed in a department that historically functioned on autocratic principles, that department would likely undergo immense chaos (and lost productivity) until a reconciliation is established.

We thus address the issue of how well the supervisor matches (or "clicks") with the existing collection of employees. In some cases, a "good match" exists, but is clouded by other problems:

> In the QEG case, the middle-aged Caucasian supervisor was adequately matched in technical knowledge and managerial style with the American-born employees in his department. However, he was a poor match with the ethnically diverse foreign-born subordinates. Employees were also poorly matched to each other. After team-building to work through diversity issues, however, the organizational climate dramatically improved.
>
> The supervisor's management style was basically autocratic. Since many of the ethnically different engineers subscribed to cultural beliefs of "respecting elders" or "respecting authority," they had no significant difficulty taking instruction or direction from their supervisor. Further, since they were accustomed in their original cultures to functioning as a collective unit (rather than as individuals alone), they became a fully functioning work group.

What do you do about masked facts? There are no "prescriptions" for how organizational consultants uncover these or other masked facts that the client organization might not acknowledge. The wise consultant, however, must develop his or her own hypotheses on which organizational aspects might contain masked facts and bring these to light:

> There is an ancient Sufi tale about the mullah (teacher) Nasrudin who is looking under a streetlight for something. One of his disciples approaches him and asks, "Oh mullah, what are you doing?" The mullah replies, "I've lost my key and I'm looking for it!" The disciple says, "Master, why don't you look here in the bushes?" Exasperated, Nasrudin admonishes him, "How can I look there, stupid? There is no light there!"

Chapter III
Establishing Causes:
How to Use Survey Instruments and Structured Interviews in Organizational Analysis

Determining *why* a symptom exists and *what* the underlying causes of problems are comprise the most difficult parts of the assessment process. These determinations are also the most crucial: *Unless we can identify the causes, we cannot help solve the organization's problems*!

Causation analysis takes different forms and requires different approaches and expertise. In the assessment process, it is often necessary to include specialty experts such as accountants, computer analysts, industrial engineers, psychologists, statisticians and others. In some cases, a team of consultants is the best approach. The approaches required for specialized assessments, such as a financial analysis, fall outside the scope of this book. For our purposes, we present a practical organizational assessment approach that, in our work, has been extremely useful in identifying basic management problems.

We use two primary assessment techniques, *survey instruments* and *structured interviews*. Either type can be used alone, or both types used together. As a general rule, *surveys used alone can identify trends in the organization's procedures or practices*. However, surveys may not provide adequate information to identify specific underlying causes or management practices that have significant impact in the work environment. The use of *structured interviews with individuals can detect unacknowledged problems*. In order to obtain the most complete and useful information, we recommend supplementing surveys with interview information.

The Use of Questionnaires and Surveys

Formal surveys are preconstructed published questionnaires that are completed by persons from whom we want feedback on general or specific areas of concern. In most cases, the survey instrument has been developed through research with an identified reference group or groups; has been analyzed statistically for validity and reliability; has a user-friendly scoring system; and comes with a manual to assist the investigator with methods of interpreting survey results.

In behavioral research, most of these surveys are viewed as "objective" tests because of their simplicity of scoring, quantifiability, derivation of statistical or actuarial data, ease of comparing similarities and/or differences between groups, and ease translating information into graphs or charts. These characteristics render surveys very practical tools when numerous employees, or employee groups, are asked to respond to the survey questionnaires.

How are surveys structured? Many surveys use numbers across a range of responses from an extreme negative end (e.g., 0 to indicate "never") to an extreme positive point (e.g., 5 to indicate "always"). Names for scales or scores vary, but the structure remains essentially the same. This type of scale (called a Likert scale) might include response scales such as the following two examples:

Exhibit 1. Sample Survey Response Scales

Scale Type 1: Agree-Disagree

0	1	2	3	4	5
STD	D	SD	SA	A	STA
strongly disagree	*disagree*	*somewhat disagree*	*somewhat agree*	*agree*	*strongly agree*

Scale Type 2: Never-Always

0	1	2	3	4	5
N	AN	R	ST	AA	A
never	*almost never*	*rarely*	*sometimes*	*almost always*	*always*

These types of surveys typically contain questions designed to elicit responses tailored to the scale choices. For example, an organizational climate survey that uses the agree-disagree scale might include items such as this:

Exhibit 2. Sample Organizational Survey Items

Using the scale below, please answer the following questions by circling the number that best represents your choice:

0	1	2	3	4	5
strongly disagree	disagree	somewhat disagree	somewhat agree	agree	strongly agree

In our organization ...
1. We are not afraid to speak our minds ...   0   1   2   3   4   5
2. We cooperate with each other ...   0   1   2   3   4   5

How are completed surveys analyzed? Most published surveys come with an instructional manual that offers methods of analyzing completed surveys. Some surveys have built-in data-analysis methods that can be purchased as accompanying software, or surveys can be sent to the publishing company for data analysis. These options are generally most cost-effective if large numbers of employees are surveyed, or if results are required as quickly as possible. In either case, computerized analysis might or might not be desirable, depending on the organization's needs or budget allotted for the organizational assessment.

We use a straightforward, economical approach to data analysis: On completion of all surveys, the results for each item are tabulated into group scores, such as a *mean* (or average) score.[1] Using this approach, we can choose any item or set of items and subject them to data analysis through a published spreadsheet program relatively quickly.

---

[1]Surveys using Likert-scale construction lend themselves easily to data input and analysis with personal computer software such as the Microsoft *Excel*™ spreadsheet program.

For example, in the Susan Donnelley case, question #1 resulted in an *actual group mean* of 1.9 on the Likert 6-point scale noted above. The mean obtained from this employee group was clearly lower than the *theoretical mean* (2.5 — midway between "0", *strongly disagree* and "5", *strongly agree*). Additionally, this group mean deviated even further from the *reference sample mean* (3.2) provided in the survey administration manual. The group average score (1.9) indicated that group members tended to "somewhat disagree" on the statement "We are not afraid to speak our minds." In other words, employees were actually afraid of speaking their minds!

Following data analysis, we can then interpret (i.e., discuss) the results of each item in the questionnaire, each category of items, or each section covering different aspects of organizational assessment. We find that written descriptions of high- and low-scoring items are most meaningful to management. Having this summary information, management can then consider alternatives to address problem areas with a substantial degree of confidence.

What are the disadvantages of using surveys/questionnaires? While surveys can be very useful, disadvantages do exist. Many people do not like preprinted surveys for various reasons:

1. They seem impersonal.
2. Questions will be interpreted according to each individual's viewpoint.
3. Some questions might be not relevant to the organization or group using the survey.
4. Extremes on the response continuum can influence the participant's choices.
5. Some individuals do not complete all items within a survey.
6. Others can vent their underlying unhappiness with the organization by writing angry notes in the margins, rather than make a choice they feel is forced upon them.
7. Still others refuse to respond, by turning in a blank survey or not turning one in at all!

Confidentiality and privacy administering surveys: To prevent potential problems, surveys should be administered in an environment of confidentiality and trust. *Confidentiality* must be addressed at the outset by carefully explaining to respondents the actual reasons and purposes of the survey, that all material is handled and/or reviewed only by designated persons, that data is analyzed by groups, and that interested persons will receive a summary of the results when available. These and other similar statements must be communicated so that respondents are assured that their participation (or how they answer the survey) is not linked with their job security.

Issues of confidentiality can also be a problem when individuals are asked to complete certain sections of the survey instrument. Surveys usually have a demographic information section, which some respondents view as information that can identify them easily. Here, it is important that individual names are not written in, so that confidentiality and privacy of the respondent is protected. The use of an identification number is typically more acceptable, and in fact can encourage respondents to answer survey questions in an open and frank manner.

Many surveys have an open-ended *comments section* at the end of the questionnaire. Respondents' handwritten comments often provide useful feedback information, or reveal emotional states or the negative bias of the writer. Some respondents do not write comments for fear of being identified by their handwriting, or see comments as an unnecessary redundancy, or feel that their statements have no true impact on the way things are done in the organization.

In other words, survey administrators must provide a clear picture of *why* the survey is being conducted, *where* the survey will take place, *who* will see survey results, *what* information will be derived from the survey, *how* the survey information will be used, and *when* results will be available. By clearly communicating these aspects at the beginning, survey administrators encourage respondents to be more cooperative.

How to Conduct Interviews and Analyze Interview Content

Why interview? Structured or semi-structured interviewing is a technique used in many social sciences for research and evaluation. Interviews provide revealing information and serve as diagnostic tools. An appropriately designed interview can:

1. Provide a qualitative rather than a quantitative "reality check" about organizational functioning.
2. Utilize person-to-person interaction in examining respondents' perceptions.

3. Offer an opportunity for the respondent to discuss his or her views, opinions, concerns, suggestions for change, and other information relevant to the employee's status in the organization.
4. Reveal how an employee relates to his or her work environment, and how the organizational culture impacts on the individual.
5. Elicit information that corroborates or nullifies other data the consultant has collected about the organization.

Thus, interviews reveal a great deal of useful information. If the consultant uses interview methods, thoughtful consideration should be given to important factors discussed below.

What are the objectives of interviews in this assessment? Before embarking on interviews, we discuss the goals or outcomes from the use of interviews with executives and with participants. With senior management, we present and discuss two major rationales for using interviews: (1) to verify general results or specific concerns obtained from the surveys; and (2) to gather additional detailed information so that we (consultants) can fully understand underlying organizational problems.

With employees who are selected to participate in interviews, we clearly define purposes and objectives in relation to existing symptoms for which the organizational assessment was originally requested. If workable, we hold this discussion in a general meeting with the identified employee group early in the consultation process. If a group meeting is not workable, we discuss objectives and purposes at the outset of each interview.

It is also important, incidentally, to *discuss what the interviews do not do*. In this regard, we discourage immediately any perception that interviews are used in negative or ethically improper ways. Thus, *interviews do not*:

- Address psychological motivations or counsel disenchanted individuals
- Serve as employee performance evaluations
- Exploit information given in confidential discussion with the "expert" or consultant
- "Spy" on employees

Confidentiality: The key to successful interviewing. As is the case when employees answer a survey questionnaire, issues of confidentiality and privacy arise immediately when an employee expects to be interviewed. These issues become even more complicated during interview sessions, and must be addressed before any formal interviews are conducted.

First, *management must be clear that any and all information shared in any interview is confidential*; the information should be held in trust between the interviewer and the employee. If management objects to this basic premise, any interviews held with subordinates can be sabotaged at the outset. The consultant must explain that he or she will summarize interview content only after all interviews have been conducted, and that the summaries will present information in a meaningful and practical manner to assist in later stages of consultation.

Second, the *employees chosen (or those who volunteer) to be interviewed must be assured of complete privacy and confidentiality*. This assurance can include the venue of interviews; interviews held in a private conference room or office away from the daily work environment will reinforce confidentiality, whereas those held in an area within the departmental workspace or in a hallway might be seen as being of questionable confidentiality. We place high value on an employee's ideas, and reinforce again and again the importance of privacy in order to obtain the most honest, thorough, and useful information possible. Confidentiality must be stressed at the beginning and at the end of any interview.

Who should be interviewed? If the client organization requests that *all persons taking the survey* are to be interviewed, the consultant must insist on a specific realistic number of persons to be interviewed due to cost/benefit limits such as scheduling the time and place for interviews, the employees' willingness to participate in interviews, and the organization's agreement to pay fees charged for the effort. Obviously, interviews with 50 persons pose far fewer difficulties than those with 500 persons!

The consultant's selection of interviewees depends on several factors, but the most important one involves objectives:

- *If the objective is to verify or to clarify survey findings, a representative sample of respondents can be selected*. One approach we have found most useful is to randomly select a predetermined number (e.g., percentage) of individuals from those who completed the organizational assessment survey and schedule them for face-to-face interviews with the consultant.
- *If the objective is to provide a forum for safe, private discussion* with persons who feel an urgency to share confidential information or to allow certain employees an opportunity to vent their frustrations without fear, these persons can be interviewed if agreement to do so has been reached between management and the consultant.

What is the structure of the interview? For our organizational assessments, we structure our interviews ahead of time so that there is consistency across interviews conducted with all selected respondents. Additionally, if more than one interviewer meets with respondents, the use of the same or similar structure permits sensible organizing of information obtained from all interviews.

The most useful structure is a set of questions or items for discussion based on results of the survey instrument. Questions the interviewer raises should be couched in an "open-ended" format. That is, avoid questions that would elicit a "yes" or "no" response. The same applies to questions that might elicit "true" or "false" responses. If the interviewer is interested in obtaining rich information, questions should allow the respondent ample opportunity to describe or to elaborate on his or her views. See Appendix 3 for sample interview items.

The structured interview lasts approximately 45 minutes. Some persons are hesitant to speak, are ordinarily not very verbal, or otherwise do not take up the entire time period. Other individuals are quite talkative and might be difficult to stop. It is important, however, to clearly indicate time limits at the beginning of the interview.

In the interview proper, we first engage the respondent by discussing or elaborating on certain survey findings. As the respondent speaks, we "follow" his or her lead while keeping in mind the essence of our previously structured interview questions.

To illustrate a structured interview between our consultant, Eric Perkins (Eric), and an employee (EMP), we present an example from the above survey finding of the low score on the item "We are not afraid to speak our minds":

Exhibit 3. Sample Structured Interview

Eric: Good morning, Mr. Emp. Thanks for coming. As you know, I've been asked to evaluate why things are they way they are in the legal department. As a worker in this department, your views are extremely important. By the way, we appreciate your cooperation with the Organization Survey, which employees took about two weeks ago. Every piece of information contributes to a better understanding of the problems in the department.

I also want to assure you that all information shared with me, either through the surveys or interviews, is completely confidential. What I share with upper management are trends I notice in people's responses. No individual's specific comments will ever be told to any superior in the company.

Now, before I begin with specific items, do you have any questions or concerns you would like to express at this time?

Emp: Well, I've been concerned myself about how other people in the department have been talking about our manager [*employee elaborates in substantial detail here*].

Eric: I'm glad you brought that up. This is precisely what I'm concerned about in the department. As I discussed in our group meeting, the survey shows that people are actually afraid to speak up with the manager. How do you personally feel about this? Can you tell me more about what people are saying?

You don't have to use names. Remember, I'd like you to know that whatever you share with me here stays here, stays with me.

Emp: [*makes comments*]

Eric: Thank you. I have a series of other questions, most based on results of the Organization Survey. As you know, I presented the general findings in a meeting last week to employees in the department.

Emp: Yes, I know. You know, I had problems with some of the questions there. I know you covered that in the discussion, but I can't help saying that a lot of my answers were on the negative side. I know I wasn't alone in answering that way. I just didn't want to say anything in the large group meeting.

Eric: Mr. Emp, you have been most helpful. I now understand better how it is for *you* as you go about your work each day. We've discussed a lot of important points. Are there any concerns you have about what we've talked over?

Emp: Not really. I'm glad we had this opportunity.

Eric: Before you leave, again, be assured that our conversation is held in the strictest confidence. Privacy is something I cherish very much personally. In my work as a management consultant, I am bound by a professional code of ethics to maintain confidentiality. If I speak or write on anything from my interviews, that information will be shared only in general terms. No one's name will be used in any reports I make. Thanks again. I'll be around next week. If there are issues that come up that you think are important, be sure to let me know.

Establishing Causes

The interviewer continued listening carefully as the employee made comments or responded to interview questions. The interviewer was alert to the interviewee's nonverbal behavior and body language, to the emotions behind the statements, and to the employee's frustrations. The interviewer made sure that the employee's responses were respected and acknowledged. Occasionally, the interviewer wrote a few notes. He assured the employee that no one would see his notes; if necessary, he showed them to the respondent.

Toward the end of the interview, the consultant took time to reassure the employee that comments were strictly confidential. If the respondent appeared unsure or troubled by the contents of the interview, the consultant took time and care to reduce anxiety or discomfort as much as possible. He also indicated when he would be around so that the employee could speak with him again if she or he had further concerns or questions about the interview process.

How should the interviewer present himself (herself) in interviews? Some individuals will view the interview with suspicion (e.g., "It is something else management is trying, but how useful will it be in the long run?" "What difference does my personal opinion make in the whole scheme of things?"). By the time of the interviews, members of the identified group might be quite wary of the consultant, might have developed shared attitudes and thoughts through discussions they have had with one another over coffee or lunch, and might have questioned more intensely management's purposes for interviews.

Thus, the consultant must show that he or she is *sincerely interested* in the respondents' opinions and views. In conjunction with this, the interviewer must *maintain a position of neutrality (or objectivity)* as much as possible. Presenting oneself as genuinely interested in the respondent and his or her concerns while not taking sides facilitates an atmosphere of "trust," the key to obtaining useful interview information.

Second, the interviewer must *demonstrate active listening*. This involves paying close attention to both verbal statements and nonverbal behavior. Throughout the interview, the respondent's physical posture, gestures, silences, erratic glances, voice tone and quality, etc. might represent his or her level of comfort or unease, signs of stress, motivations, hidden meanings, and other important unstated attitudes.

An experienced interviewer can quickly detect inconsistencies between the respondent's statements (verbal behavior) and his or her underlying attitudes (seen in nonverbal behavior). In other words, you, the interviewer, will learn more by listening than by talking. Through actively listening, you will learn possible sources of organizational problems and have a rich opportunity to silently assess the respondent and to determine the truthfulness of his or her statements.

What if personal problems emerge during the interview? Good question. Interviewing employees in an organizational assessment might take on characteristics of counseling sessions if the interviewer is not attentive to this possibility. This is one reason why the predetermined structure is important: A useful structure minimizes or prevents the use of the interview as a counseling session. Nevertheless, despite safeguards, one or more individuals will discuss their personal problems or personality conflicts with co-workers, or focus on problems they have outside the workplace.

Should highly personal material arise in the course of the interview, a useful rule-of-thumb is to ask the respondent, "How has [this] affected your work performance? How does [this] affect your relationships at work?" or raise similar items to discuss. This strategy re-focuses the respondent toward the workplace and the actual purposes of the interview.

If you determine that personal material is relevant to the organizational assessment, it must be incorporated into your investigation. For example, if the department manager were a difficult, demanding, irrational, or unreasonable person, most underlings would have trouble coping with the boss' unpredictability. During an interview, an employee might exhibit severe stress reactions, depression, anxiety, loss of self-esteem, or other highly personal material associated with working under a difficult manager.

In some cases, presentation of personal material indicates deeper psychological-social-personal problems that are the province of professional therapists. These individuals should be referred, of course, to the employee assistance counselor in the organization, or to an outside licensed therapist. Such recommendations must be made in complete confidence, and this special confidential information must be reinforced with the employee before the end of the interview session.

What can you learn from interviews that you do not learn from surveys? As an alternate investigative technique, *interviewing often identifies issues or problems that cannot be obtained through a formal survey instrument.* Published surveys might not contain specific questions unique to the organization or the department being evaluated. Responses to some survey questions can also be diluted or glossed over by responses to other questions.

Establishing Causes 35

For example, in the Susan Donnelley case, one of the issues that arose from interviews was an accusation that she discriminated against ethnic minority workers. Ten workers in confidential interviews (10 out of 80 employees, or 12.5%) lodged this allegation. On closer inspection, we found that the 10 interview respondents actually represented 70% of the minority employees in the entire organization!

In vivid contrast, the corresponding item in the formal survey (which all employees were asked to complete) resulted in a "no problem" rating. Thus, even if the minority employees rated the racial discrimination item as "somewhat a problem" to "definitely a problem", their responses to that survey item were masked by the "no problem" responses given by nonminority (i.e., the majority of) employees.

The interview procedure thus clearly identified the manager's discriminatory behaviors. This useful information implied potential legal, managerial, and organizational problems that could have resulted if they had not been addressed. Furthermore, the organization's image in the community and its public relations efforts were potentially compromised by this underlying discrimination the manager communicated toward minority employees.

How are interview results analyzed? The analysis of interview responses begins with *categorizing interview content*. Categories include specific content, how often participants bring up particular issues, and how elaborate their responses are. Each issue is assigned a value from "0" to "10," where "0" represents "no concern" and "10" represents "major concern."

After interview content is categorized, the categories themselves can be subjected to simple statistical analysis (e.g. an estimate of how often, or how many employees reported the same dimensions). The simplest meaningful statistics include averages and percentages on a content category. In turn, the statistical information can be translated into bar graphs or other visual charts.

The Use of Supervisor-Subordinate Data to Demonstrate Causation

In the Susan Donnelley case, we identified Susan's leadership skills and managerial practices as key causes of problems within her department. Because of the department's important role in the organization, Susan's leadership problems potentially affected the entire company! At this point, the consultant reviewed assessment findings with senior management and recommended additional assessment.

In this phase, we next sought answers to the question "Why does she have these leadership problems?" To investigate this, we used a *leadership questionnaire:* one form administered to Susan, a second form to all her subordinates. We could then compare the manager's perception of her leadership skills to the subordinates' (hereafter indicated as SUBS) perceptions.

This type of comparison can be called a "revealed differences" approach: We present manager data alongside subordinates' data in visual table or chart format during discussion of assessment results. The resulting presentation has remarkable effects on educating management about causation, in team building training, and in clarifying skills with the identified problem manager.

In Susan's case, she rated herself "high" in all leadership skill categories. Her SUBS ranked her "low" on the same dimensions. Thus, she felt she was a good manager while her SUBS felt the opposite. Our analysis of specific subcategories clearly indicated vast differences in perception:

Exhibit 4. Comparison of Subordinates' Ratings with Manager's Ratings on Leadership Skills

Leadership Skills[1]	SUBS' Ratings	Susan's Ratings
accepting new ideas	1.8	3.7
communication skills	1.5	3.0
soliciting trust	2.8	4.8
interpersonal relations	2.3	4.0
rewarding good performance	1.4	2.3

By definition, leadership skills involve a manager's personal self-awareness, control needs, concerns about decision-making, skill in dealing with criticism, and skills in interacting in a superior-subordinate relationship. Taking a look at these data, Susan's subordinates clearly perceived her leadership skills very differently than Susan herself did! Their low rankings on her leadership skills explained the increasing negative feelings in

---

[1]The leadership skills represent those found in the actual survey instrument. They are renamed only for demonstration purposes in this section.

subordinates. This negativism further exacerbated ongoing problems in the department. In turn, Susan became more defensive and autocratic.

The results of the subordinate and manager leadership surveys indicated a need for additional private interviews with Susan. We first reviewed with her the subordinates' mean ratings and how those differed from her own ratings. Seeing this data and discussing its implications with the consultant, she was able to understand more clearly how she came across to employees. Further, at our encouragement, Susan spent one day in intensive leadership training with our leadership and psychological specialist. Additional individual interviews with Susan were conducted on an as-needed basis. In our follow-up phase, we reviewed with Susan the progress on specific departmental factors and her leadership skills.

Chapter IV
Evaluating Alternatives

In organizations, as in society itself, "people-problems" involve many variables that impact on the "people-in-an-organization" environment. As we stated elsewhere in this book, we believe that *all problems in organizations involve the complex interaction of people in the organization.*

Before evaluating alternatives, the wise organization should have determined sensible *criteria* to use during the actual evaluation process. At a minimum, the following criteria should be essential characteristics of viable alternatives:

- alternatives must be realistic in terms of cost, risk, and legal/ethical consideration
- alternatives must be cost effective
- alternatives must contain one or more trade-offs

Three Easy Steps for Evaluating Alternatives. Any alternative has its own set of pros and cons or advantages and disadvantages. These must be weighed carefully while evaluating alternatives. To simply list the pros and cons and then arrive at conclusions that "sound good" does not truly address long-term problems. Rather, this approach often remedies problems on a short-term basis only — a band-aid patch up when organizational surgery might be needed.

We propose a three-step approach for increasing objectivity while evaluating alternatives:

1. List all alternatives in a clear and concise visual format (e.g., chart).
2. List pros and cons under each alternative.
3. Assign a risk value to each pro and con reason.

Typically, the first two steps are readily defined by the organization having difficulties. Step three, assigning risk values, is discussed in detail here. A *risk value* is a specific positive weight or negative weight assigned to advantages and disadvantages of any alternative. Risk values serve as indicators of factors such as costs/benefits, trade-offs, risks to the organization, potential legal problems, and possible ethical issues. Each of these factors can be viewed as having positive values or negative values, which can later be added together to arrive at an overall risk value. Using a mathematical type model, our risk value equation is illustrated below:

Exhibit 5. Risk Value Equation

Risk Value = (cost/benefit analysis) + (trade-offs) + (organizational risk) + (legal considerations) + (ethical factors)

To simplify this step, we use a risk values table presented in Exhibit 6.

**Exhibit 6. Risk Values Table
To Evaluate Pros and Cons of Alternatives**

Risk factors	*Code*
High financial cost if implemented =	-1C
Zero/lower cost if implemented =	+1C
High tradeoff =	+1T
Zero/low tradeoff =	-1T
High risk to organization =	-1R
Zero/low risk to organization =	+1R
High legal potential =	-1L
Zero/low legal potential =	+1L
High ethical problem =	-1E
Zero/low ethical problem =	+1E

How to Evaluate Alternatives when Leadership is the Problem

The ability to manage people and to interact in productive ways are desirable qualities that all managers ought to possess. Ideally, pre-employment interviews and information gathering should determine whether an individual will be a good "match" with the employees he or she will be working with. Unfortunately, organizations often assume, mistakenly so, that an individual's technical expertise is synonymous with leadership abilities. Thus the axiom "The best engineers make the best managers" is in fact false!

In Susan Donnelley's case, for example, she was an outstanding lawyer and expert in contract law. In the previous chapter, we demonstrated that her managerial/leadership skills were assessed by her subordinates as *average* or *well below average* depending on the skill area. At the same time, however, she rated herself as *well above average* in the same areas. Clearly, these very different views accounted for much of the chaos and problems in Susan's department.

More importantly, the results of the organizational assessment forced upper management to confront the problems: "What should we do about Susan? We cannot simply allow the situation to continue! What alternatives should we consider?"

To demonstrate our approach, we again use the Susan Donnelley example. In step one, the consultant and upper management developed a list of six alternatives:

Exhibit 7. Alternatives Re: Susan Donnelley

1. Terminate Susan's employment.
2. Transfer her to another unit of the organization as a manager.
3. Promote her to a higher level position.
4. Remove her as manager but retain her as a technical expert.
5. Give her training and counseling, and retain her as manager.
6. Place her on probation as a manager, pending results of the training and counseling program.

Obviously, each of these alternatives rendered its own set of pros and cons or advantages and disadvantages. After listing the pros and cons, we considered and tabulated the costs (e.g., risks) for each by using the risk values table. In the example below, note that the weights for the cons column total -11 even though only 6 disadvantages are listed. The use of weighted values demonstrates risks concisely and efficiently.

Exhibit 8. Sample Risk Values
Alternative #1 – *"Terminate Susan's Employment"*

Pros/Advantages	Value	Cons/Disadvantages	Value
1. Eliminates existing problems immediately.	+1T	1. She will file legal action re: wrongful discharge, racial/gender discrimination.	-1L -1C -1T
2. Employees will see that upper management takes problems/complaints seriously.	+1T	2. We will lose her technical expertise.	-1R -1T
3. Other managers will see the results of poor managerial or leadership behaviors.	+1T	3. We admit to failure to provide her with proper support and training.	-1R -1R
		4. Women/minority employees might show negative reactions.	
		5. There might be negative publicity in the media.	-1R -1C -1R -1C
		6. The organization's reputation in the industry might be compromised.	
total risk values	**+3**		**-11**

By subjecting each alternative to this procedure, the organization can arrive at the most realistic and appropriate solution(s). In turn, the top three alternatives can be offered and discussed with the manager, who can assist in selecting the final alternative to be implemented if she is to be involved.

Special Considerations Regarding the Manager's Ability to Manage. Many problems relating to managing people and interacting in productive relationships can be minimized or eliminated before they arise by determining whether an individual is suitable to be a manager.

One common assumption is that technical expertise assures managerial ability. This assumption has been negated in almost all studies of leadership. The personality characteristics of a high level technician (e.g., what makes this individual an outstanding technician) are not, in most cases, correlated with good managerial characteristics. The belief that "The best engineer makes the best manager," for example, is simply not true! While there are exceptions, the best engineer should remain the best engineer!

In Susan's case, she was an outstanding lawyer and expert in contract law. Unfortunately, she reached a compensation impasse as her career progressed: The road to higher pay (e.g., advancement) required Susan to become a manager. Taking this route, Susan nearly failed in her first year as manager! A better option would be for upper management to adjust compensation scales to assure that technical expertise is not penalized but is rewarded the same way good management is.

In the next chapter, we address the fifth step in the assessment process — the selection of the best solution, given the environment in which the organization operates.

Chapter V
Selecting the Optimum Solution

As we state elsewhere in this book, organizational assessment helps identify general and specific problems and assists in developing recommendations for problem resolution. We also noted earlier that recommendations and their alternatives must be carefully considered. In this chapter, we discuss both short-range and long-range recommendations.

Short-range solutions are actions that can be implemented immediately, have short timelines, and generally have low or minimum costs. In some situations, they are necessary so that crucial issues can be rectified immediately rather than further delayed. Examples of short-range solutions include replacing a manager, implementing focused team-building in a particular work group, transferring an employee to another department, or purchasing new and much needed equipment.

On the other hand, *long-range solutions* are actions that involve longer timelines, require substantive or additional analysis, may have variable costs that need to be examined against the company's annual budget, or have a long-term preventative objective. These may include replacing outdated manufacturing methods with current technology, developing an international marketing strategy, or obtaining new and expanded work space as the company grows.

To demonstrate short-term and long-term solutions, we refer again to the Susan Donnelley case in which we had conducted an extensive organizational assessment. For the problems we identified, the following recommendations were submitted:

Exhibit 9. Short-Range Recommendations Regarding Susan Donnelley

Recommendations	Justification
1. To achieve positive leadership and effective management in the shortest possible time, appoint a deputy manager to assist the department manager in the administration of the department. With this appointment, managerial roles/tasks for each position should be clearly defined: Separate out administrative and technical functions.	1. The department manager currently has eleven unit supervisors reporting to her. Each supervisor represents specialized technical service areas. This span of control in the department is too large for one manager. Also, the manager's "open door" policy has increased role conflict/role ambiguity among employees and supervisors, which has created accountability and performance problems.
2. Provide intensive and specific training for all department management personnel — supervisory, interpersonal, diversity, communications, and conflict resolution skills.	2. The leadership surveys showed that all supervisors received low (below average) ratings from subordinates. Specific areas included ineffective communications, poor interpersonal interaction, inadequate conflict resolution skills, and insensitivity to diversity issues.
3. Counseling for the department manager to be provided by a licensed clinical psychologist who specializes in work stress, work-related psycho-social issues, managerial and leadership skills training, executive coaching, and interpersonal therapy.	3. Both the survey and interview assessments indicated that the department manager had considerable difficulty interacting with subordinates, peers, and customers. The manager's behavior gave confusing or "mixed" messages to others and contributed to reduced employee motivation, increased intergroup conflicts, customer complaints, and difficulty interacting with her superiors.

Selecting the Optimum Solution

Exhibit 10. Long-Range Recommendations Regarding Susan Donnelley

Recommendations	Justification
1. Focused team-building sessions with all department employees to address specific problems: moral, intergroup relations, diversity, communications, and organizational performance. This recommendation would require an extended time period. Abbreviated team-building should be conducted at six-month intervals for reinforcement.	1. Findings from both the surveys and interviews indicated high job dissatisfaction, lack of adequate interpersonal skills among managers, employee role conflicts/ambiguity, disregard for diversity. Fact analysis showed increased turnover rate in the prior six months for this department (above-average expectations for similar departments in the company).
2. Conduct a comprehensive work-flow analysis to assess the work process itself.	2. Assessment results indicated difficulties and ambiguities in the work process. Additionally, the original assessment contract did not include a comprehensive analysis of tasks, coordination, structure, and sequence of the work performed — all of which would pinpoint where the difficulties and problems in work process lie.

Chapter VI
Presenting Results

Now that the organizational assessment has been completed, the next step is to present the findings and recommended solutions to management. We use two basic elements in this process: The verbal presentation and the written presentation.

Verbal Presentations. Results and recommendations can be presented to one individual or to a group. In some cases, both individual and group presentations are essential. Regardless of to whom the consultant presents findings and recommendations, we consider the presentation objectives: Is the presentation to a chief executive officer, who wants only a 15-minute briefing? Is it to a group of managers on assessment details? Is the presentation an informative educational discussion to line employees? In any case, it is important to include physical (i.e., hard copy) data or information that recipients can visually see and/or take away with them at the end of the presentation.

Brief short presentations to an executive officer ought to include a bullet page or an outline that states key facts and findings (See Appendix 4 for a sample Brief Executive Summary Report). The bullets serve as reference points as the consultant and executive discuss each point in as much detail as desired by the client executive. This page can be presented on a standard 8.5" x 11" paper or on a small presentation stand.

Verbal-Visual Presentations. For presentations to larger groups, a large chart or overhead transparency slide is a more appropriate visual aid. If the consultant wishes to prepare a computer-generated presentation (i.e., Power Point™), it is often an even more effective, easy to understand visual aid.

In a group presentation, the amount of detail presented must be adjusted to accomplish the stated objective of the presentation. Typically, with middle or first-line managers, findings and recommendations are tailored to their daily functions. This is particularly important if recommendations require specific actions or changes by them.

The length of the presentation ought to be carefully controlled so that recipients gain sufficient understanding of summaries of the results, do not lose interest in the meeting, and are not separated from their daily work for extended periods of time.

Written Presentations or Reports. A written report of the organizational assessment, findings, and recommendations is generally required as part of the consultant's contract. However, even when client organizations do not require this product, it is a very useful feature of the consultation process. The objective of the written report is to provide the details of all aspects of the project, from inception to its conclusion.

These details include assessment procedures, findings, and recommendations supported by the consultant's observations, survey and/or interview results, statistical analysis of data (if applicable), interpretation of findings, and other relevant information. The amount of detail should be related to the client's needs, the organization's capability to act on the recommendations, justification for selecting optimum alternatives, cost/benefit considerations, and other relevant aspects.

In many cases, the initial consulting arrangement stipulates the level and type of detail required. For our Susan Donnelley consultation, the client executives stipulated their reporting requirements. Here, we included survey statistical details for each unit in the organization. These details were arranged in table form and were presented in appendices at the end of the primary report.

We recommend that written reports be presented in two parts: An *Executive Summary* and a full *Organizational Assessment Primary Report*. The first is an elaboration of the bulleted one-page summary used in discussion with the executive. We prefer to have a completed Executive Summary ready to be given to the client at the end of the brief verbal presentation, as described above. This Executive Summary should also be included in the full report.

The *Organizational Assessment Primary Report* presents the details of the different phases of assessment. In the Susan Donnelley case, for example, the full report contained two parts: Part I exhibited the Executive Summary, while Part II contained the details. An outline of that report is illustrated in Appendix 5.

Other Reporting Considerations. While we recognize that reports will vary in length and complexity, we feel it is vitally important to present a written report as an attractive and high-quality product. To this end, we make sure that the report is free of typographical errors, that fonts used are consistent throughout, that any graphics or charts are arranged clearly and are pertinent to their sections, and that the pages are clean and not smudged.

Often, photocopies of short reports meet our quality requirements. For multiple copies of long detailed reports, we have them reproduced and bound by a local printing service. The printing/publication costs should be built into the original contracting fees and agreed upon by both the client and the consultant.

Other related aspects that the consultant should honor include submission of the number and types of reports on the date originally agreed upon. Last but not least, confidentiality regarding any information obtained throughout the consulting project must be maintained and protected.

Chapter VII
Other Considerations

Any details and implications of an engagement should be considered carefully by the consultant in his or her efforts to conduct a successful organizational assessment. This chapter discusses additional issues pertinent to all assessment projects, but not necessarily part of the technical details of the assessment. These aspects include scope of consultation, client expectations, consultant expectations, and consulting fees.

Scope of Consultation. Scope refers to the explicit parameters and constraints of those processes or services that are included and those that are not included in the projects. In other words, determine what the boundaries of the assessment are. For example, if the assignment is to "perform an analysis of the personnel selection system," the scope must include a precise description of the elements of the system to be examined.

In our experience, we had one case in which the engagement was based on the use of two specific organizational survey instruments identified in the original contract. Our fee and timelines were based on the use of these surveys. Partway through the project, the client wanted to add a comprehensive psychological instrument to the assessment. The inclusion of this instrument would have involved the services of a licensed psychologist, the purchase of tests from the publisher, costs for computer scoring services, and other details that needed to be worked out. The additional costs for products and subcontractor services and sudden imposition on the current organizational assessment project rendered this additional request unworkable. The client soon agreed that this should be handled as a separate engagement.

Client Expectations. Related to scope of consultation, the consultant might need to evaluate *how realistic the client's expectations are* in the first meeting. Some executives present nearly impossible, if not impractical, expectations for an organizational assessment. Other executives present such an extremely narrow view that the assessment would likely not produce enough information to use in developing recommendations for addressing problems.

Because a consultant is an "outside expert," the client organization might view him or her as a rescuer, an all-knowing oracle, an unbiased professional who will produce results as management envisions, a problem solver, or even a magician! Any mythical expectations attributed to the consultant must be dispelled as quickly as possible. At the same time, realistic expectations can be reinforced or defined by the consultant in the first meeting.

An example of ill-defined expectations came from a colleague who phoned us for help. After conducting an organizational assessment, he presented his findings and recommendations. In the midst of the discussion, the client abruptly informed him that this was not what he had asked for. After the consultant reviewed the terms of his contract, he discovered that the project's scope was so ambiguous that several interpretations of what was to be included and excluded were possible. This vaguely worded contract further indicated to the consultant that he had failed to reinforce his understanding of the project's scope (and thereby the client's expectations) as he submitted progress reports to management. Had he included his framework during each phase of the engagement, major misunderstandings would have been caught well before completion of the assessment.

Consultant Expectations. In the first meeting with management, consultants expect to obtain sufficient information to develop an assessment plan. For some engagements, part of the consultant's responsibility (which is reflected in his or her fees) is time spent on reviewing the systems within the organization to become better informed about the company and thereby expedite formulation of an assessment plan.

Regardless of whether or not the consultant needs to do background research, his or her expectations about the project must be articulated in order to prevent misunderstanding. Expectations can range from office space to be made available to the consultant when on company grounds to who schedules appointments for employee interviews to what knowledge of additional professional or business resources is needed in the course of the project.

Progress Reports. Periodic progress reports to the client are an important aspect of the assessment engagement. Progress reports serve several purposes:

1. To inform the client on the status of the project in a timely manner.
2. To enable the consultant and client to discuss atypical or unusual problems or emerging findings.

3. To assist the consultant in formulating other options or hypotheses in the course of the engagement.
4. To note trends, dynamics, strengths, and weaknesses of the organization during each phase.
5. To identify further tasks to be completed.

In one of our projects, we used interviewing as the primary assessment technique. A number of employees made a group decision not to participate and therefore did not keep scheduled appointments. In this project, we were required to submit a progress report each morning after we arrived on site. We, of course, discussed employee absences with the client. Working together with the client, we arrived at a different approach to obtain the needed information to complete the project without losing time or momentum.

In another case, while conducting an employee interview, we discovered a potentially serious problem involving sexual harassment allegations. The employee at that point was considering hiring an attorney. After obtaining a written disclosure from the employee, we discussed the matter with management, who was completely unaware of the problem. In this situation, we encouraged management to alert the employee to the in-house complaint investigation process. This action curtailed possible litigation by the employee at that point in time.

Obviously, progress reports benefit both the client and the consultant: Information shared along the way reinforces a collaborative process, maintains mutual trust, and nourishes the client-consultant relationship.

Ethics and Professional Conduct. Consultants, by and large, have standards of professional practice, or a code of conduct that they use in their professional and personal lives.[1] Many consultants who function as independent contractors subscribe to ethical principles of the professional associations to which they belong. Consulting companies frequently articulate their own set of principles of professional conduct in addition to those advocated by professional associations or societies.

We do not describe details of different ethical codes in this limited space. Rather, we caution any consultant to be alert to any of his or her behaviors that might be misunderstood; e.g., behaviors that might be perceived as "harassment" that the consultant could be liable for. These might include inappropriate treatment of organizations or persons whose race, ethnicity,

---

[1] See copy of IMC Code of Ethics in Appendix 6.

gender, abilities, disabilities, or sexual preference might be different from the consultant's.

As an example, California enacted a legal statute in 1994 to specifically apply sexual harassment laws to professionals, including physicians, lawyers, mental health workers, accountants, and others. This new law provides specific actions for victims to take against providers of service (including consultants) who allegedly violate sexual harassment laws.[1]

Confidentiality. To further reinforce the importance of ethical conduct, we pay special attention to issues of confidentiality and privacy, which we discussed earlier in Chapter IV. The cautions we cited in that chapter are worth repeating here.

In the use of survey instruments, the demographic information section and the open-ended "comments" section might be viewed by respondents as direct links or clues to their identity. Due to this possibility, we inform respondents from the outset that their names are not required, that we treat all information confidentially, that only the consultants will see the data, and that data will be reported as group data, not individual data. Further elaboration on this topic is found in Chapter III, Establishing Causes.

A special case of confidentiality is apparent whenever structured interviews are used in the assessment process. The assurance of confidentiality is crucial in obtaining open and factual information from respondents. In the course of an interview, information shared by the employee might be highly sensitive for that individual, as we noted in Chapter III. As a preventive measure, we tell management that any information obtained from individual interviews is strictly confidential. Information derived from interviews is compiled as collective or summarized data.

Regardless of the approaches used in organizational assessment, certain personal feelings and attitudes (in both the consultant and client) can emerge during the project. Unarticulated or questionable organizational procedures or other information might also arise. These unanticipated occurrences should also remain as confidential as possible.

These confidentiality requirements are established early on as part of the original consulting agreement. If special circumstances arise and confidential information given by a certain employee is needed, we obtain a signed disclosure from that individual. In the potential sexual harassment situation cited above, we obtained a signed consent to disclose information from the employee before discussing the problem with management.

---

[1] The Hayden Act (passed 9/21/94). Section 51.9 Civil Code, Chapter 710, (SB 612).

Other Considerations

The *Executive Summary Report* and the *Primary Organizational Assessment Report* are often classified by the client as "confidential." If so designated, the consultant controls the distribution of the report by submitting it only to persons identified in the contract. Additionally, we imprint the front cover of our final reports with:

CONFIDENTIAL   CONFIDENTIAL

Fees. In the crucial matter of compensation, most consulting fees are based on completion of specific tasks or phases of the project. In some cases, assessment contracts have a final cap or amount that the organization allocates to the project. This amount is stated specifically in the contract and is based on the specific tasks to be performed. Additional tasks requested by the client during the project must be handled by negotiation at the time these tasks arise. By and large, it behooves the consultant and client to define the scope of the project as precisely as possible right from the start. Certain professional organizations clearly specify the type of fee arrangements they accept.

In this chapter, we have identified special aspects of the consulting process that can "make or break" the consultant's quality of service and thereby his or her professional reputation. While these are not necessarily required elements in any engagement, we feel that consultants must be alert to them as much as possible. Further, the consistent use of these guidelines will enhance the professionalism individual consultants bring to their profession.

Chapter VIII
Case Studies

The following cases are presented to the reader to supplement his or her professional experience in organizational assessment and consultation. Sections titled "Case Issues" are designed to assist in this effort. In short, case material is designed to enhance our educational objectives:

1. To demonstrate a generic and effective approach to organizational assessment through case analysis, from identifying symptoms to making recommendations for change.
2. To illustrate the dilemmas that upper management faces with supervisor-subordinates problems.
3. To demonstrate a longitudinal perspective about a new manager of a long-standing department and its employees' response to her managerial behavior.
4. To demonstrate key roles and functions of effective management consultations.
5. To demonstrate the application of organizational and leadership survey instruments and their usefulness in defining needed changes in an organizational department.
6. To illustrate the role of structured interviews in enhancing survey findings.
7. To examine managerial leadership as perceived by subordinates and by managers themselves.
8. To raise and examine important issues of organizational functioning or malfunctioning.

In this section, we present the case of Susan Donnelley in detail. The related pertinent case, The Selection, is presented in summary form. Also included in this section are intriguing and complex cases on harassment (Chang v. Collins) and on workplace diversity (QEG). Both of these examples represent perplexing organizational problems that are likely to increase in the twenty-first century as larger numbers of women, ethnically and culturally different persons, individuals with different sexual orientations, and persons of mixed ages and social status work together in organizations.[1]

---

[1] See D. Jamieson and J. O'Mara (1991). *Managing Workforce 2000*. San Francisco: Jossey-Bass. See also J. Fernandez (1991). *Managing a Diverse Workforce*. Lexington, MA: Lexington Books.

Case Illustration: Susan Donnelley

Introduction. Susan Donnelley was appointed the new manager of Star Corporation's legal department. Approximately one year later, the vice president of Star Corporation's California division, Jason Nicholas, was seriously concerned about problems in the department. He conferred with Walter Kaminsky, Director of Human Resource Management. The following transcript describes their discussion:

Jason: Sit down, Walter. I need to discuss a major problem with you.

Walter: What's the problem?

Jason: In the last several months, I've received a lot of very negative feedback on Susan Donnelley. From all over the company. From her own people. From customers.

Walter: What kind of negative feedback?

Jason: Everything ranging from "she is an autocrat and a micro-manager" to "she is rude, vindictive, untrustworthy, unpredictable, unreliable." You name it. In short, she is considered a "lousy manager."

Walter: I have had some feedback on her but nothing that bad.

Jason: Well, we selected and appointed her. As I recall, one of the male unit chiefs filed legal action against us for discrimination in hiring. What's the status of that suit?

Walter: It started as an EEO complaint, but is now in court. We may have to settle the suit out-of court, according to our lawyers.

Jason: Why?

Walter: It will be cheaper in the long run and less newsworthy. We already had too much media publicity on this. Our lawyers don't think we can win the case—it's a jury trial, you know!

Jason: All right. Tell our lawyers to settle out of court. Now back to Susan. What are we going to do about those problems? What can we do about her?

Walter called Eric Perkins, Ph.D., CMC, and arranged an appointment. During their meeting, Dr. Perkins suggested an organizational assessment focusing on managerial and leadership performance. Arrangements were made for Eric to visit the legal department and to meet Susan Donnelley. Eric suggested that Susan's immediate superior, Jason, meet with Susan ahead of time to explain the consultant's visit. The initial meeting took place on Monday at 9:00 a.m. in the legal department conference room. Key persons in attendance were Dr. Eric Perkins, Susan Donnelley, Jason Nicholas, and Walter Kaminsky.

Jason: [After introductions ....] Welcome back, Dr. Perkins. Susan, I explained to you earlier why Dr. Perkins is here. We have a delicate situation here, and I hope he can be as helpful to us now as he has been in the past. [The group briefly discusses workers' complaints and departmental problems]. Dr. Perkins, may I ask you to lead the rest of this meeting?

Eric: Thank you. Please call me Eric. Everyone I've worked with at Star does. The situation in the legal department is not unusual for a company this size. I am sure that there are many approaches to "fixing" any organizational problem. Here, what I suggest as the first step is to conduct an assessment, an evaluation, or a diagnostic workup of why things are the way they are. For this analysis I suggest two types of surveys to evaluate people's perceptions of strengths and weaknesses in the department: A Leadership Survey and an Organization Survey.

The Leadership Survey will give us specific feedback about each manager from his or her subordinates. This survey also includes a self-assessment part that each manager completes on himself or herself. The results from both parts are later tabulated and compared. It is in the statistical comparison that we will gain useful information of how differences and similarities in perception contribute to departmental problems. The Organization Survey will give us feedback on the department as a whole: how it functions, its performance, employee perceptions and expectations, and so on.

In addition, I suggest that I personally interview randomly selected employees in the department and all supervisors.

Some questions and discussion for clarification follow. The group agrees on this approach. Arrangements are made both for administering the formal surveys and for individual interviews.

Eric: OK! It's important that workers are "prepped" for my presence. Susan, I suggest you send out a message as soon as possible to all employees in the department. Let them know I will be reviewing the productivity and effectiveness of the department. Be sure to mention the surveys and the interviews specifically.

Organizational Assessment Methods

The assessment phase required approximately four weeks' time. In this phase, we used both survey questionnaires and structured interviews.

Survey Instruments. Three surveys were administered, including the Organization Survey, the Leadership Assessment Survey, and the Supervisor/Manager Self-Survey.

The *Organization Survey* instrument was sent confidentially through office mail to all 80 members of the legal department. Respondents were asked to complete the questionnaire anonymously and return it to a central collection place. The approximate time required for completing the instrument was 30 minutes. Respondents were given two days to complete and return them. The return rate was 93% (N=74).[1]

The *Leadership Assessment Survey* instrument was administered to the subordinates of the seven managers, including Susan Donnelley's subordinates. Each group met separately with Dr. Perkins in a conference room located at the human resources department training center. He administered the questionnaires and supervised each session, which lasted approximately 30 minutes. Almost all employees (98%) completed this survey.[2]

The *Supervisor/Manager Self-Survey* was administered to the seven managers on a Saturday morning, again supervised by Dr. Perkins. This administration required 30 minutes.[3]

---

[1] M. J. O'Brien (1994). *Learning, Organization Practices Profile (LOPP)*, San Diego, CA: Pfeiffer & Co.
[2] J. M. Kouzes and B. Z. Posner (1993). *Observer Form, Leadership Practices Inventory (LPI)*, San Diego, CA: Pfeiffer & Co.
[3] Ibid. *Self-Survey Form, (LPI)*

Structured Interviews. In this engagement, all employees were given an opportunity to participate in interviews lasting 45-60 minutes. From this pool, Dr. Perkins interviewed selected members of the legal department. Two or more interviews were conducted with ten employees at their request. Interviews were arranged at a time and place that assured workers of individual privacy and confidentiality. Most interviews were held in a conference room or office away from the legal department itself.

To obtain "customer input" and for assessment control and comparison purposes, Dr. Perkins also conducted a limited number of interviews with supervisors and with employees from outside the legal department.

Organizational Assessment Findings

Results of Organizational Survey. While the survey instruments contained questions with Likert-scale choices, some respondents spontaneously wrote comments (typically hostile or negatively toned statements) in the margins of the survey. An open-ended section at the end of the instruments gave respondents an opportunity to express themselves in their own words. Most of these responses were also negative, with many comments ending with multiple exclamation marks. Exhibit A summarizes the survey categories and average scores:

Susan Donnelley
Exhibit A
Organization Survey Results

	Three Organizational Systems[1] and Their Subsystems	Subsystem Group Mean	Main System Group Mean
	The Leadership System		**2.6**
A.	Vision and Strategy	2.5	
B.	Executive Practices	2.6	
C.	Managerial Practices	2.5	
D.	Climate	2.7	
	Job Structure and Job System		**2.7**
E.	Organizational and Job Structure	2.6	
F.	Information Flow	3.1	
G.	Individual and Team Practices	2.7	
H.	Work Processes	2.5	
	Performance and Development System		**2.8**
I.	Performance Goals and Feedback	2.9	
J.	Training and Education	2.4	
K.	Rewards and Recognition	2.4	
L.	Individual and Team Development	3.5	

[1]For systems and subsystems content, see Exhibit F. Also see M.J. O'Brien (1994). *Learning Organization Practices Profile: Guide to Administration and Implementation*, San Diego, CA: Pfeiffer & Co.

This data clearly indicates that all three major organizational systems were rated relatively low by employees — below average (and below the theoretical mean of 3.0). While not significantly different from the other systems, the *Leadership System* was rated the lowest by employees.

Results of Leadership Surveys. Keeping in mind that the Leadership Practices Inventory asked subordinates to rate their immediate supervisors and asked that managers rate themselves, the leadership survey results included the following:

First, in all leadership categories, managers rated themselves 1 or more points higher, on average, than their subordinates did (Exhibit B)! In particular, managers rated themselves the highest on *enabling* others to act and *modeling* the way in their work roles. In contrast, subordinates rated all seven managers below average (2.5 mean rating out of theoretical mean of 3.0) on these dimensions. Exhibit C demonstrates the array of mean scores from both managers and subordinates in each leadership category.

Susan Donnelley
Exhibit B
Mean Ratings for All Managers by Leadership Category

Leadership Category[1]	Managers as Rated by Subordinates	Manager's Self-Rating
Challenging	2.6	3.7
Inspiring	2.2	3.2
Enabling	2.8	4.2
Modeling	2.6	4.0
Encouraging	2.4	3.4
Survey mean	2.5	3.7
Theoretical mean	3.0	3.0

---

[1]See Exhibit F for survey content. For administration guidelines, see J. M. Kouzes and B. Z. Posner (1993). *Leadership Practices Inventory: A Self-Assessment and Analysis,* San Diego, CA: Pfeiffer & Co.

Susan Donnelley
Exhibit C
Comparison of Managers' and Subordinates' Mean Ratings on Five Leadership Qualities

Leadership Category	1: Rarely or Very seldom	2: Once in a while	3: Sometimes	4: Fairly often	5: Almost always or Frequently
Challenging		S		M	
Inspiring		S		M	
Enabling		S		M	
Modeling		S		M	
Encouraging		S		M	

S = Subordinates   M = Managers   3.0 = Theoretical mean

Second, six of the seven managers acknowledged in the survey their leadership strengths (high mean scores) as well as their shortcomings (low mean scores). These are illustrated in Exhibit D. Manager #3 apparently viewed him- or herself very highly (4.4 out of a possible 5.0 score). However, this manager received a mean score of only 2.6 from subordinates (Exhibit E)! Clearly, this obviously significant difference (nearly 2 points) in perception between this manager and his or her workers implies that either some major problems exist within his or her department, or that this manager carries an elevated view of him- or herself.

Susan Donnelley
Exhibit D
**Leadership Self-Evaluation Mean Scores:
How Seven Managers Rated Themselves**

	Manager (MGR) Identification Number							
Leadership Category	1	2	3	4	5	6	7	MGR mean
Challenging	2.5	2.5	4.3	3.5	4.2	3.8	3.7	3.7
Inspiring	2.8	2.8	4.3	2.5	2.8	3.5	3.0	3.2
Enabling	4.5	4.5	4.5	4.8	3.2	4.2	4.8	4.2
Modeling	3.5	3.5	4.5	4.5	3.8	4.2	4.0	4.0
Encouraging	3.5	3.3	4.3	4.0	3.0	3.7	2.3	3.0
MGR mean	3.4	3.3	4.4	3.9	3.4	3.9	3.6	3.7
Theoretical mean	3.0	3.0	3.0	3.0	3.0	3.0	3.0	3.0

Susan Donnelley — Exhibit E
**Leadership Observer Mean Scores:
How Subordinates Rated Their Managers**

	Manager Identification Number							
Leadership Category	1	2	3	4	5	6	7	MGR mean
Challenging	3.0	2.3	2.8	2.3	3.0	3.0	1.8	**2.6**
Inspiring	2.7	1.7	2.3	2.0	2.2	2.5	1.5	**2.2**
Enabling	2.8	2.4	2.0	3.0	3.0	2.7	2.8	**2.8**
Modeling	2.7	2.6	2.7	2.8	2.8	2.5	2.3	**2.6**
Encouraging	2.8	2.3	3.0	2.8	2.2	2.5	1.4	**2.4**
MGR mean	2.8	2.3	2.6	2.6	2.6	2.6	2.0	2.5
Theoretical mean	3.0	3.0	3.0	3.0	3.0	3.0	3.0	3.0

Case Studies

In Susan Donnelley's case (Manager #7), she rated herself at a survey mean of 3.6, above the theoretical mean of 3.0. Susan's subordinates rated her with a survey mean of 2.0, a little more than 1-1/2 points difference. It is noteworthy that the subordinates' survey mean score was the lowest given to any of the managers (Exhibit E). This finding is consistent with the initial concerns expressed by upper management: Susan's workers were restless, stressed, and frustrated with Susan's management of the department.

Susan Donnelley
Exhibit F
Five Leader Characteristics
Defined in the Leadership Practices Inventory[1]

---

1. **Challenging the Process.** Leaders are persons who seek out new opportunities, innovate, experiment, take risks, and explore ways to improve the organization.

2. **Inspiring a Shared Vision.** Leaders envision a future with a positive and hopeful outlook, are expressive, attract followers, have skillful communications, and show others how mutual interests are met through commitment to common purpose.

3. **Enabling Others to Act.** Leaders develop relationships with mutual trust, stress collaborative goals, involve others in planning, encourage decision-making, and ensure that others feel strong and capable.

4. **Modeling the Way.** Leaders are clear about their business values and beliefs, keep on course, model how they expect others to act, plan projects in achievable steps, create opportunities, and focus on key priorities.

5. **Encouraging the Heart.** Leaders recognize and find ways to celebrate accomplishments, encourage people to persist in their efforts, let people know their efforts are appreciated, show pride in the team's achievements, and nurture team spirit.

---

[1] J. M. Kouzes and B. Z. Posner (1993). *Leadership Practices Inventory (LPI)*, San Diego, CA: Pfeiffer & Co. See also J. M. Kouzes and B. Z. Posner (1987). *The Leadership Challenge: How to Get Extraordinary Things Done in Organizations.* San Francisco: Jossey-Bass.

Interview Results

Individual interviews with selected members of the legal department were analyzed in terms of both nonverbal behavior and interview content. Behaviorally, some respondents were anxious in their behavior or demonstrated little or no trust in the interview process. For example:

- Several employees appeared for interviews but refused to participate.
- Some employees hesitated to enter the interview room; others talked in subdued voice; still others made sure the door was closed tight, or otherwise appeared restless or uncomfortable.
- Most employees required continued assurance of confidentiality during the interview.

When we analyzed interview content, we relegated specific content into categories and rated them according to frequency of occurrence, from high occurrence (assigned a score of "10") to low occurrence (score of "1"). Exhibit G illustrates summaries of most frequently occurring categories; phrases in italics are actual comments made by respondents.

Susan Donnelley
Exhibit G
Interview Content Categories[1]

Rank		Frequency of Occurrence
1.	Problems with leadership and management — *micro management, no people skills, poor role model, managers project negativism*	10
2.	Communications problems — *nobody knows what's going on, no consultation, no communication, no staff meetings*	10
3.	Workload distribution — *heavy for some, nothing to do for others, used as retaliation by managers*	9
4.	Chain of command problems — *supervisors are bypassed, no delegation, conflicting instructions*	9
5.	Lack of strategic vision and objectives — *no clear objectives, people don't know what's going on, goals not communicated*	9
6.	Problems in organizational culture — *supervisors are not technically qualified, no standard approach, constant change*	8
7.	Discrimination — *ethnic/gender bias, favoritism, fairness problem, use assignments to retaliate*	7
8.	Lack of advancement opportunities — *no training available, no promotions, many people are leaving*	7
9.	Lack of rewards and recognition — *supervisors do not appreciate our work, no awards, no bonuses*	6

Interview material thus reinforced organizational systems that employees had rated low (i.e. major problems) in the formal organizational survey.

Lastly, the limited interviews with supervisors and employees from outside the legal department demonstrated "mixed" results. That is, some interviewees had high opinions while others had low or no opinions of the legal department and how it was managed. However, all interviewees felt that Susan Donnelley as a manager was *not as good a manager* as was the former (retired) head of the department. The majority also felt that service to the corporation by the department had deteriorated under Susan's leadership.

---

[1]The consultant labeled the content categories; respondents' actual phrases are shown in italics.

Case Summary

In this case, we were called in to help the Star Corporation's upper management understand what was going on in their legal department in order to make recommendations for remedial action. Our surveys, both organization and leadership, helped identify and define departmental problems more accurately than if our analysis had been based solely on workers' complaints, behaviors, productivity problems, and other symptoms experienced over many months. Further, structured interviews clarified and enriched our work as consultants to this very troubled department.

Case Issues/Questions

1. What are the key problems in this case? Describe symptoms and possible causes.
2. What immediate action, if any, should management take about Susan? About her performance?
3. What action should be taken by management about the low ratings subordinates gave to their supervisors?
4. Prepare a plan for management to resolve leadership problems in the department. Also include in this plan the next steps to be taken regarding other problems disclosed by the organizational survey.

A Brief Analysis of the Susan Donnelley Case
Sequence of Events Summary

1. Star Corporation engages a consultant from outside the company.
2. The consultant and associates perform organizational assessment and leadership surveys with department employees. Consultant also conducts structured interviews with employees and selected customers.
3. Surveys reveal major problems in organizational performance, motivation, job satisfaction levels, and significant differences in perception of leadership by managers and subordinates.
4. Consultant presents findings and recommendations to upper management and selected findings to legal department employees.

Case Studies

Step 1. Identifying Symptoms

1. Negative feedback from "customer."
2. Dissatisfaction and low morale in the department, affecting performance.

Step 2. Establishing the Facts

1. Susan was appointed as the new manager of the legal department one year ago.
2. Senior management failed to use an effective, appropriate, and fair selection process for hiring Susan Donnelley as manager.
3. Susan's appointment as manager was questioned by other qualified individuals.
4. Legal action is currently pending regarding discriminatory hiring with Susan's appointment.
5. The company's vice president heard negative comments regarding Susan's management and leadership style.
6. Management did not have an effective mentoring program for new managers.
7. No structured management training programs or opportunities were available, especially for managers new to the company or a particular division.
8. Definitions of managers' and supervisors' responsibilities and authority were ambiguous.
9. Managers in general lacked knowledge and understanding of how their subordinates perceived them as leaders.

Step 3. Establishing Causes

1. The Organizational Survey indicated that employees rated all organizational systems as below average (theoretical mean = 3.0).
   - Leadership System was rated at 2.6
   - Job Structure and Job System was rated at 2.7
   - Performance and Development System at 2.8

2. On the Leadership Practices Inventory, all participating managers rated themselves significantly higher than subordinates rated them.

3. On the Leadership Practices Inventory, Susan Donnelley received the lowest overall ratings of all the managers.
4. Interview material indicated that employees perceived serious problems with organizational culture, lack of advancement opportunities, lack of rewards and recognition, and worker bias. Many of Susan's subordinates perceived her as having a strong need to control, emphasizing micro-management methods, and using an autocratic management style.

Step 4. Evaluating Alternatives

Short-term Solutions

1. Transfer Susan.
2. Terminate Susan.
3. Promote Susan to a higher level (e.g., a staff appointment).
4. Provide counseling to Susan.
5. Provide management training, especially team-building.
6. Change Susan's status from manager to a technical position (staff expert).
7. Change organizational structure to include a deputy manager; define specific responsibility and authority.

Long-term Solutions

1. Review selection, mentoring, and training process and programs.
2. Review problem areas identified in organization survey and interviewing.
3. Set up team-building sessions for managers and employee groups to improve communication; address conflict issues and diversity problems; and improve group participation within work groups, with managers, and with customers.
4. Develop a feedback system for employees (e.g., ombudsmen).
5. Reassess results of changes within six months of completing each recommended task.

Step 5. Selecting Optimum Solutions

Short-term Solutions

1. Provide counseling to Susan and to selected managers.
2. Conduct immediate team-building for all managers and all employee groups.
3. Appoint deputy manager; establish and define responsibilities and authority of all managers.

Long-term Solutions

1. All alternatives listed are recommended.
2. Team-building to be continued on a scheduled basis to promote continual reinforcement.

Actual Outcome

The Star Corporation accepted all but two recommendations we presented. In place of the recommendations to appoint a deputy manager and the use of an ombudsman, the department was restructured to reduce the span of control for Susan and a more efficient feedback system was set up. Six months after the presentation of recommendations, all tasks had been implemented or were progressing on schedule (long-term).

The Selection

Introduction. The Star Corporation is a multidivisional corporation with divisions in Virginia, Utah, California, and Washington. Products manufactured by the company are primarily electronic components used by the aerospace industry in aircraft, space vehicles, and military weapons systems. Each division operates as an independent profit center, with performance accountability controlled by the headquarters division, located in Falls Church, Virginia.

The Utah division is located in Salt Lake City; the California division is located in San Jose, and the Washington division is located in Tacoma. The Corporation's affirmative action policies articulate a commitment to diversity.

Alfonse Rossini was the manager of the legal department of the Star Corporation's California division for twenty-one years. When he retired, division management appointed Donald Drake, one of three unit chiefs in the legal department, as interim manager pending the selection of a new head for the department.

The Company Hires a New Manager. After Rossini's retirement, the California division sent an "Open Position" notice for a new manager of the legal department to all Star Corporation divisions. Position announcements were also published in the *Wall Street Journal* and various professional publications. As a result of this effort, thirty-nine applications were received.

The human resource management department performed a preliminary screening of the applicants. It should be noted that all supervisory personnel were graduate attorneys and members of the state bar in the states where their divisions were located. The screening eliminated those candidates who had no relevant experience, who were not members of the California bar, whose law degrees were from nonaccredited institutions, or who did not have adequate technical expertise. This screening eliminated all but ten applicants.

The ten applicant-files were sent to the division vice president's office for review. That review produced a "short list" of five final applicants. Three of the five finalists were Star Corporation employees; the other two were from outside the Corporation.

Donald Drake, interim manager, was one of the five final applicants. He was a 57-year-old Caucasian with extensive technical expertise. He had been with the Star Corporation for fifteen years, and served in the Washington and Utah divisions before his promotion to unit chief in California. Drake held a BS degree in Electrical Engineering and a JD degree from the University of

Southern California. He was the only applicant from the California division.

The five final applicants were invited to San Jose for personal interviews. After the interviews were completed, Susan Donnelley was selected as the manager of the legal department. Susan Donnelley had been a branch manager in the legal department of the headquarters division in Virginia. She was 46 years old, an ethnic minority woman, and had been with the company for eight years. She held a BA degree and a J.D. degree from Stanford University, and an MBA from the University of Richmond in Virginia. She was a member of the California Bar and the Virginia Bar.

Problems with the Manager Selection Process. Two days after the appointment of Susan Donnelley was announced, Donald Drake asked for an appointment with Jason Nicholas, vice president of the California division. The appointment was scheduled for later that day. Drake arrived at the Administration Building and was shown into the VP's office by the secretary. The following transcript describes their meeting:

Jason: Hello, Don. What can I do for you?

Donald: I wanted to talk to you about the new department manager appointment.

Jason: Yes? What about it?

Donald: I want to know why I was not selected. Surely, I was well qualified.

Jason: Yes, I had expected this conversation. Let me say first that all five finalists demonstrated excellent credentials and background, including you. We appointed Susan Donnelley for several reasons: (1) Ms. Donnelley had the best credentials; (2) We need to appoint more minority individuals to high level positions; (3) We need to appoint more women into upper management; and (4) She has more time left in her career then you do.

Donald: You mean to tell me that she was picked over me because she is a minority woman and younger than I am?

Jason: We followed the company's affirmative action policies and other personnel regulations. I went over my final decision with the personnel people and they were happy with it.

Donald Well, I am not happy with it! [Drake leaves abruptly.]

Two weeks later, the Star Corporation was informed by the Equal Employment Opportunity Commission (EEOC) that Donald Drake had filed a formal complaint with the Commission for the following alleged violations: *racial discrimination, gender discrimination,* and *age discrimination*. In addition, the Corporation was contacted separately by Donald Drake's attorneys and was informed that charges were being filed in state court for *breach of contract, harassment,* and *emotional distress,* as well as other related but unspecified charges.

Case Issues

1. What violations of Donald Drake's rights as an employee, if any, were committed by the Star Corporation?
2. What federal and state statutes are involved?
3. What other options are available to Donald Drake?
4. What management and personnel problems does this case present for the Star Corporation?
5. Develop a plan of action for the Star Corporation to deal with the allegations stated in the EEOC and state complaints.

References

1. The Civil Rights Act of 1964, as amended (Title VII).

2. The California Fair Employment and Housing Act.

3. The Civil Rights Act of 1991.

4. Executive Order 11246.

5. The Age Discrimination in Employment Act of 1967 (ADEA).

Case Studies

The Selection
Exhibit A
Star Corporation Legal Department's Organizational Structure

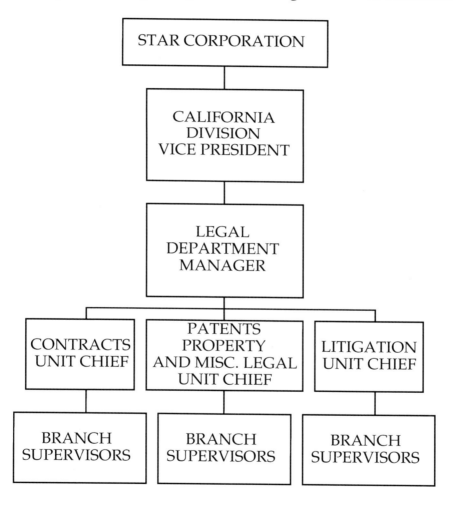

Case Study: Chang versus Collins

Introduction: Pam and Bill. William Collins and Pamela Chang worked in the California division of the Star Corporation (see The Selection for a description of the Star Corporation). At the time of this case, both were production planning specialists in the manufacturing department's production planning and scheduling unit.

William (Bill) Collins has been with the Star Corporation for twenty years in various positions. Bill has a high school education and has served four years in the U.S. Navy. He is 43 years old, Caucasian, married, and has three children ages 8, 13, and 15. Bill was born in Los Angeles, California.

Pamela (Pam) Chang has been with the Star Corporation for five years. She worked with the U.S. Army Corps of Engineers before joining Star. She received a B.S. degree in Mechanical Engineering from San Jose State University in San Jose, California. At the time of the case, she was 29 years old, Asian American, and unmarried. Pam was born in Taiwan and came to the U.S. when she was 6 years old. She lives with her parents.

Both Pam and Bill worked in the same unit. Pam had been assigned to the unit three months before the consultant was called in. Their office arrangement was an open area with six-foot-high partitions between work groups and hallways. Pam's desk was near the exit. Bill's was behind and to the right of Pam's (Exhibit A).

**Exhibit A
Work Area Layout**

Case Studies

The Problem: Workplace Harassment. Jane Rossiter is a personnel specialist in the human resources department of Star Corporation. She is one of several HRM coordinators, one serving each department in the division. Her specific duties are to coordinate complaints involving racial, sexual, gender, and ethnic harassment filed by employees of the division. Jane's responsibilities include the manufacturing department.

One afternoon Jane received a call from Pamela Chang, asking for an appointment. When Pam arrived, she appeared overtly distressed:

Jane	Pam, what's going on?
Pam	I can't take it anymore!
Jane:	Why don't you tell me about it?
Pam:	For the last three months, Bill Collins has been harassing me every day. I can't do my work. He calls me at home. Leaves little packages on my desk. Puts his hand on my neck when he walks by.
Jane:	Have you reported this to your supervisor?
Pam:	No! Bill is one of Karl's buddies. They were in the Navy together.
Jane	Have you told Bill to stop it?
Pam:	Yes! Every time it happens! When he calls me at home, I tell him to stop it and hang up. In the office, I try to avoid him even though that's difficult because he sits behind me and I know he stares at me all the time. I returned all the packages he leaves on my desk. Everybody in the unit knows about it. The men laugh and think it's funny. The women told me to report him. I am reporting him now. That's why I'm here!
Jane:	OK. I'll take care of it.

After Pam left, Jane saw Larry Starling, her immediate supervisor and manager of the employee relations unit. After discussing Pam's case with Larry, he decided to use the "outside investigator" option of their Employee Complaint/Grievance Procedure because of the apparent seriousness of the allegations and the potential bias inherent in using a company investigator.

Larry contacted Michael Harrington, JD, Ph.D., an independent consultant who is an expert in discrimination and harassment issues. Harrington had also consulted with Star Corporation's California division in the past. He holds degrees in both law and organizational psychology and is the author of several published articles on racial and sexual harassment.

The Consultant's Findings. Michael Harrington arrived at the California division's headquarters on Monday morning. A private office had been arranged for him. As requested by Mike, interviews were scheduled with Pam Chang; Bill Collins; their supervisor, Karl Benning; and other employees who worked in the same office area.

Interview with Pamela Chang. The interview information was essentially the same as Pam had reported earlier to Jane Rossiter.

Interview with Bill Collins. Bill arrives and enters the private office set aside for Mike:

Bill: I'm Bill Collins. What do I call you? Dr. Harrington?

Mike: Doc. The people here usually call me Doc.

Bill: OK, Doc. I know why I've been told to come here. That woman is lying. I have never harassed her. She has been giving me the eye ever since I was assigned to this work area. I just picked up on it.

Mike: What do you mean, "She's been giving me the eye"?

Bill: Oh, you know how women are, Doc. They wink at you, smile at you, and wiggle their behinds.

Mike: Has she ever said anything specific to you? That you thought was interesting?

Bill: She didn't have to. I can tell when a woman is interested in me.

Mike: What about the packages you gave her and what about the claim that you touched her?

Bill: What packages? I never gave her anything. I never touched her!

Mike: What about the phone calls to her home?

Bill: What phone calls? I never called her at home!

Mike: Why do you think she filed the complaint against you?

Bill: You of all people should know why, Doc. She's a frustrated woman. She's 29 years old and not married. She's an engineer; she thinks she's better than the rest of us who don't have engineering degrees. She's a minority; she thinks she deserves special treatment. This is her way of getting attention from management — maybe a promotion. You know, Doc, I've had it with this mess. I might just file a complaint against her for character assassination and causing me trouble at work. If my wife ever finds out about this, I'm going to have trouble at home too. My wife is from Alabama. You understand what I mean?

Later that day, Bill Collins filed a complaint with the human resources department against Pamela Collins for *harassment, character assassination*, and *defamation*.

Interview with Karl Benning, Supervisor. Karl stated he was not aware of any problems between Pam Chang and Bill Collins. Neither had spoken with him about any difficulties. His office was not in the general work area in which Pam and Bill were situated. He went to their area only when necessary for work-related reasons.

Interviews with Co-Workers. Mike Harrington interviewed individually six male and four female co-workers (see Exhibit B). None of the males felt that the interaction between Pam and Bill was "unusual" or "harassing." Of the four female employees interviewed, one felt that Bill "paid too much attention" to Pam. One of the women felt that Pam was instigating most of the interaction between herself and Bill. The other two women stated that they were not aware of anything unusual. None of the women admitted to advising Pam to file a formal complaint.

Case Issues

1. What are the facts in this case? What corroboration exists to sustain the allegations by Pam? The denials by Bill?
2. What specific immediate action should be taken at this time by management?
3. What actions should be taken by management regarding the complaint by Pam? The counter-complaint by Bill?
4. What cross-cultural and/or culture-specific issues are present in this case?
5. Prepare a report to management detailing your assessment, conclusions, and recommendations to resolve this case.

Chang versus Collins
Exhibit B
Characteristics of Production Planning Unit Personnel

Name	position	years with company	education	age	race/ethnicity	sex
Karl	Supervisor	20	BS, Engineering	50	Caucasian	M
Joan	Secretary	3	High School	22	Caucasian	F
Joe	PPS V	9	BS, Eng., MBA	37	Caucasian	M
Pam	PPS IV	5	BS, Engineering	29	Asian-Am	F
Bill	PPS III	20	High School	43	Caucasian	M
John	PPS III	20	High School	45	African-Am	M
Maria	PPS III	10	BA, Business	36	Hispanic-Am	F
Carlos	PPS II	15	High School	40	Hispanic-Am	M
Peter	PPS II	3	BS, Engineering	27	Asian-Am	M
Vicky	PPS I	1	BS, Business	23	Caucasian	F

Case Study: The Quality Engineering Group (QEG)

Introduction: Diversity in the Workplace. The QEG is the quality engineering group in the engineering department of Tellus Corporation. The Tellus Corporation is a government contractor, primarily engaged in Department of Defense (DOD) contracts for designing and manufacturing military aircraft weapons systems. The QEG has the responsibility of developing and designing the quality engineering specifications for these systems.

The group consists of fourteen employees and a supervisor. The group is unique because of the members' diverse racial, ethnic, cultural, and religious backgrounds:

- 3 foreign-born Vietnamese females
- 3 foreign-born Vietnamese males
- 1 foreign-born Pakistani Muslim male
- 1 foreign-born Asian-Indian Hindu male
- 1 U.S.-born Hispanic-American male
- 1 U.S.-born African-American male
- 3 U.S.-born Caucasian males
- 2 U.S.-born Caucasian females

In this group, twelve individuals were graduate engineers with degrees from U.S. universities; two (the Hindu and Muslim men) received their engineering degrees in other countries. All engineers were considered competent professionals as indicated by their "average" or "above average" performance evaluations. One of the U.S.-born females was the unit secretary. Demographic details of the unit members are presented in Exhibits A and B.

The supervisor, Bill Watson, a 49-year-old Caucasian male, had been transferred to this position six months prior to our consultation project with the group. He had been a supervisor for fifteen years in other engineering groups in the Tellus Corporation. He had had no previous experience supervising a group as culturally diverse as the QEG.

Tellus Corporation has a company policy that requires all employees to attend a one-hour diversity training seminar every two years. An outside consulting firm conducts the seminar. The training consists of a thirty-minute videotape that covers general topics related to racial, ethnic, and gender statistics in the U.S. and a thirty-minute question-and-answer period after employees viewed the tape. All QEG members had completed this seminar.

QEG
Exhibit A
QEG Personnel Demographic Characteristics

	Name*	Job Classification	Position	Co. Yrs.	Sex	Age	Ethnicity	Yrs. in U.S.
1.	Bill W.	Supervisor	Supervisor	20	M	49	C –NB	
2.	Diane Y.	Secretary III	Secretary	15	F	49	C –NB	
3.	Janet N.	Engineer IV	Lead Eng.	10	F	37	V –FB	15
4.	Alvin A.	Engineer II	Engineer	3	M	26	AFA –NB	
5.	Carol P.	Engineer II	Engineer	5	F	28	V –FB	8
6.	Jack K.	Engineer III	Engineer	9	M	55	AI –FB	23
7.	Jim K.	Engineer II	Engineer	4	M	29	V –FB	10
8.	John Y.	Engineer I	Engineer	2	M	25	V –FB	6
9.	Mike R.	Engineer III	Engineer	8	M	37	C –NB	
10.	Mustafa M.	Engineer III	Engineer	8	M	52	V –FB	20
11.	Paul S.	Engineer II	Engineer	3	M	27	HA –NB	
12.	Phillis B.	Engineer II	Engineer	3	F	29	C –NB	
13.	Susan K.	Engineer II	Engineer	5	F	27	V –FB	8
14.	Tom S.	Engineer III	Engineer	9	M	34	C –NB	
15.	William W.	Engineer I	Engineer	2	M	25	V -FB	7

*Foreign-born persons frequently use American/English first names for easier pronunciation by Americans and Westerners. The first three, all of whom have administrative responsibilities, are listed by position. Other employees are listed alphabetically by first name.

Legend:
Co. yrs = number of years with Tellus Corporation
AFA = African-American
Yrs. in U.S. = number of years in
US AI = Asian, Indian, Hindu American
C = Caucasian
NB = Native (American)-born
HA = Hispanic-American
FB = foreign-born
V = Vietnamese

Case Studies

The Case. Bob McArthur, director of engineering, had just returned from a weeklong trip to Washington, D.C., where he had been conferring with Department of Defense (DOD) representatives on the XM-2 project. As he walked into his office, his secretary met him with an urgent message from Joe Rizzo, Tellus' manager of the XM-2 project. "Need to see you immediately!" was the message. Bob asked his secretary to have him come in, which Joe did within five minutes. Their discussion transpired as follows:

Bob: Hi, Joe! OK, what's so urgent? I just got back today from D.C.

Joe: I know. Sorry to put this on you so quickly. We have a BIG problem with the quality specs on the XM-2.

Bob: What's the problem? I just saw the DOD people on this project.

Joe: I just found out about it from my design people less than an hour ago. The specs are all screwed up. The estimates are too low for the stress factors in the system.

Bob: Have you talked with the supervisor? What's his position on this?

Joe: Yes! He doesn't know what's going on.

Bob then immediately calls Bill Watson, the QEG supervisor, to come in immediately to see him:

Bob: Bill, what's going on with the specs on XM-2?

Bill: I've been checking the specs myself since Joe called this morning. They are way off! I've been talking with my engineers, but all I get is double talk about problems with the Vietnamese lead engineer, Janet, and with Mustafa, who is handling most of this project.

Bob: What kind of problem? What's going on with Janet? With Mustafa?

Bill: I don't know. The Vietnamese talk to each other in Vietnamese. No one in the group, except for the Americans, speaks English well enough for me to know what's going on. Most of the time, I don't know whether my instructions are understood. They just nod their heads when I talk to them. I don't get it. They've been here long enough to speak English. At least they seem to read it well enough.

Bob: You've been with the group what, about six months? Why hasn't this come up before? I never knew you had this kind of problem. Basic language problems. This is serious. It seriously affects technical work, doesn't it? We've got to figure out what to do about this. Let me talk with the vice-president. Meanwhile, continue to check the specs and get them corrected as soon as possible.

QEG
Exhibit B
Additional Background Information on Selected Workers

Name	Janet K.	Bill Watson	Mustafa M.	Jack K.
Education	BS, Chem Engr., Ohio State U.; MS, Indus. Engr., U. Pittsburgh	BS, Mech. Engr., U. Missouri	BS, Mech. Engr., Inst. of Tech. (Germany)	BS, Elec. Engr., Punjab U. (India)
No. Years with Tellus	10	20	8	9
Rank: most recent eval.*	8	9	7	7
National Origin	Vietnam	U.S.	Pakistan	India
Native and other languages	Vietnamese, some English	American English	Pakistani dialect, some German, French, English	Hindi, Urdu, some English
Spoken English**	3	—	4	4
Written English**	8	—	6	6
Religion	Buddhist	Protestant	Muslim	Hindu
Marital status, other	divorced: lives with 2 children ages 10 and 3	married: no minor children	married: 4 children ages 5-18; owns local grocery store, staffed by family workers	married: no minor children

*most recent performance evaluation: 1 =low 10 =high
**facility in English — spoken or written: 1 =low 10 =high

Bob met with the division vice president later that day. A group as diverse as the QEG immediately signaled interpersonal and cross-cultural problems, misunderstood or minimally understood communications, and other potential undefined problems that would have to be dealt with as quickly as possible. Tellus could not risk jeopardizing a multi-million dollar DOD contract if one of its main engineering groups had problems working as a team — let alone making technical mistakes in specifications. The two of them decided the best approach would be to bring in an outside management consultant experienced with diversity issues to conduct an organizational assessment.

The Consultant and the Assessment Findings. The Benham Consulting Group was selected for this project. One of their chief consultants, Peter Ritter, Ph.D., had performed several assignments with Tellus Corporation in past years. He was familiar with the company, with its products, and with its people. He was well respected at Tellus for his previous work, his tact, and for his ability to get things done effectively.

Peter Ritter arrived early one Monday morning to meet with Bob McArthur and Bill Watson. On hearing some details of the group's problems, Peter recommended an organizational assessment that used structured interviews with all employees in the QEG, with Joe Rizzo, manager of the XM-2 project, and with selected other personnel within Tellus Corporation. Additionally, Peter suggested a preliminary work-flow analysis of the group's activities.

Results of Work-Flow Analysis. The preliminary work-flow analysis revealed a cumbersome and inefficient process of assigning, scheduling, and executing tasks. There were numerous duplications and overlaps of tasks and assignments. An evaluation of project deadlines showed that 80% of the group's required project completion deadlines were not met.

Results of Interviews with the QEG Personnel. Significant social problems emerged, as indicated by the following:

1. *Stable Cliques*. Several cliques existed in the group: One consisted of the three Vietnamese males, one consisted of the two Vietnamese females, and another consisted of the three Caucasian engineers. The other engineers (including Janet, the Vietnamese lead engineer) were not involved in any of the cliques.
2. *Poor Supervisory Leadership*. Most members of the group considered the supervisor, Bill Watts, a poor leader. He was described as *aloof, disinterested, biased in handing out assignments, and unable to complete his work.*

3. *A Mismatched Team.* The lead engineer, Janet (Vietnamese female), was put in charge of the team assigned to the XM-2 project: Mustafa (Muslim male), Jack K. (Hindu male), two Vietnamese females, and John Y. (Vietnamese male).
4. *Language Barriers.* The Vietnamese workers often used their native language while working. Non-Vietnamese workers felt (and complained) that this was *rude and inappropriate,* and *interfered* with work tasks.
5. *Preferential Treatment.* Caucasian engineers felt that the nonwhite workers received preferential treatment from the supervisor in work assignments.
6. *Social Rejection.* The lead engineer, Janet, was disliked by everyone in the group, but was considered technically competent and a "good engineer." She was described as *arrogant and abrasive, rude, aggressive, and authoritative*
7. *Competition and Hostility.* Janet and Mustafa apparently interacted with a great deal of hostility toward one another. Mustafa refused to accept instructions or orders from Janet, the lead engineer. Although not as intense, similar responses came from Jack K. (Hindu).
8. *The Company's Ethnic Nightmare.* Interviews with other personnel in the Tellus Corporation indicated that the group was difficult to work with: They missed deadlines consistently, their language differences created major problems in technical and interpersonal communication, and some QEG engineers demonstrated serious difficulties with English language usage.

Main Issues

Clearly, multiple problems existed within this work group. Main issues could be addressed by asking variations of a single generic question, "What should be done about….?"

1. The composition of the current XM-2 project team?
2. The different cliques in the QEG?
3. The use of foreign languages in the workplace?
4. The poor command of English by foreign-born workers?
5. The complaint of "preferential treatment" ?
6. The supervisor, Bill Watson?
7. The lead engineer, Janet?
8. Mustafa and Jack K.?
9. Hostility between Mustafa and Janet and between Jack K. and Janet?
10. Other apparent hostile interactions among other workers?
11. The problems with work flow, failure to meet deadlines, task inefficiencies, and other work process problems?

Case Study: Western Tire and Alignment, Inc.
Part A

Introduction: Description of Company. Western Tire and Alignment, Inc. (WTA) is a privately owned company that offers tires and alignment services to retail customers, commercial customers (car dealers, construction companies), and government agencies (police/sheriffs' departments, fire departments). WTA's competition includes eight other tire businesses, most of them associated with large national tire chains or national retail stores (Sears, Wal-Mart).

WTA has five retail service stores located in different towns within a fifty-mile radius of Center City, where the company's headquarters and stores are located. The total number of full-time employees is approximately 100, and a varied number of seasonal workers are hired as needed.

Two basic services are provided by WTA: tire sales and installation, and brake repair and alignment. These services are processed as follows:

1. *Sales and installation of new tires* – The store manager takes the order, reviews the daily schedule, and gives the customer an estimate of time required to perform the service. In general, most customers can be accommodated on the same day for both purchase and installation, due to WTA's in-stock inventory of most major tire brands (Michelin™, General™, Bridgestone™, etc.).

    Special requests for nonstocked or unusual tires (i.e., special brands, high performance tires) are special-ordered through a distributor or manufacturer. It takes several days' to obtain special-order tires, and customers are scheduled for subsequent dates of service. Commercial and governmental customers, large trucks, and construction equipment are serviced by appointment only.

2. *Brakes and Alignment* – Certified mechanics perform limited mechanical services: brakes, alignments, shocks, wheels, lube and oil changes, and related special services. A separate area in each store contains several bays with hydraulic lifts, pits, and alignment equipment. WTA does not perform engine repairs, general vehicle diagnostic services, or electrical system repairs.

The standard organization of a store consists of a store manager, an assistant manager, one to three mechanics, and three to twelve "tire busters," depending on the store size. "Tire busters" are employees who remove old tires and place new ones on vehicles. The minimum requirements for this position include a valid state driver's license and the physical ability to lift and move tires. There are no female tire busters or mechanics in any of the stores; apparently, no woman has ever applied for a tire buster position.

WTA offers competitive salaries: Store managers are paid a salary plus bonuses based on the annual profit performance of each manager's store. WTA pays tire busters above-average wages compared to similar jobs in competitor businesses. Mechanics are paid below prevailing per-hour union scale wages (WTA employees are not unionized). Mechanics also receive a commission based on performance and volume. All employees receive substantive benefits: A health plan, retirement plan, sick leave, and an annual vacation.

The Case: WTA's Salmon Creek Store

Introduction. Salmon Creek is a city of approximately 45,000 and is located fifty miles from Center City. Salmon Creek is the site of a large state prison, a hospital, a community college, and a state university. The city has no major industrial companies.

Among the five WTA stores, the Salmon Creek Store (SCS) possesses unique characteristics:

- The competitive environment in Salmon Creek is more pronounced than in the other four locations (e.g., a larger number of competitive tire stores exists in Salmon Creek than in the other cities).
- Most of the business in the SCS is retail. The SCS has few government customers, car dealerships, or construction company customers.
- The SCS is the largest store in size and in number of employees.
- SCS has three managers (an owner-store manager, a service manager, and an assistant manager, see Exhibit A). The four other stores have a two-manager structure (store manager and assistant manager).

History of the Salmon Creek Store. The SCS store has been in business for many years and has been located in its present site for over thirty years. Fred Denton had held the position of store manager at Salmon Creek for twenty years. Don Hagan had been the assistant manager for five years.

Case Studies

The unique organizational structure at the SCS originated two years ago when Joe Martin became a partner in WTA. Joe had owned and operated his own tire store for twenty years in Salmon Creek. During a period of economic recession in the area, Joe's business suffered severe losses, and he sold his inventory, equipment, and building to WTA. Joe's store was located in a part of the city some distance from WTA's Salmon Creek store. As part of the acquisition agreement, Joe was invited to buy a 10% ownership in WTA and was appointed store manager of the SCS.

Abrupt Changes in the SCS Management Structure. The news about the new ownership and management structure at the store came as a shock to some employees: The acquisition of Joe's store had been treated as a confidential transaction by the owners of WTA. The merger was scheduled for a formal announcement to all managers and employees on July 15.

At 8:00 A.M. on July 14, a Monday morning, the new minority owner, Joe Martin, walked into the SCS and announced that he was the *new owner/manager of the store!* The current managers, Fred and Don, stared at him in disbelief. One of the majority owners, Mr. Bianci, was present at the time and confirmed Joe's ownership and the change in management structure. The major owners each now owned 45%, while Joe owned 10% of WTA.

Fred and Don asked immediately for a meeting with the two majority owners, Mr. Bianci and Mr. Steiger. At the meeting, both were ostensibly angry and demanded to know what was going on. "Why weren't we told of the changes? Where do we stand now under the new arrangement?" Bianci and Steiger stated that they felt they had acted in the best interest of WTA, that the new management structure was part of the acquisition, and that they did not owe justifications or explanations to anyone about how they ran their company. They further stated that both Fred and Don would remain as managers at the SCS, and that Joe would be an "owner-manager."

Salmon Creek's Decline: Management Calls in a Consultant. During the two years following the change, conditions at the SCS deteriorated significantly. Profitability decreased 30% by the end of the second year. Employee turnover increased by 50%. Morale problems among the SCS employees increased: Shouting matches between Fred and Joe occurred almost daily. Employee hostility, bickering, and tardiness commonly occurred. Customers increasingly complained about declining quality of service, problems with scheduling, foul language, and rude and unprofessional behavior by employees.

WTA
Exhibit A
Salmon Creek Store Managers' Biographical Information

Joe Martin *Owner-Manager*	Age 59. Owned his own tire store for twenty years. Worked for several large tire manufacturers as a sales representative for several years prior to opening his own business. Born in Los Angeles. High school diploma. Married. One daughter, now age 30. Enjoys old movies. Plays trumpet in local jazz band on weekends as a hobby.
Fred Denton *Service Manager*	Age 45. Has worked for WTA for twenty-five years after serving two years in U.S. Army. No other past employment. Born in Tulsa, Oklahoma. High school diploma. Divorced and remarried. Three grown children from first marriage. No children from second marriage. Enjoys hiking and camping.
Don Hagan *Assistant Manager*	Age 36. Has been with WTA seven years. Worked as a mechanic for several large car dealerships throughout the country. Has Associate degree in Automotive Mechanics. Served four years in U.S. Navy. Married. No children. Works on racing cars as a hobby.

In the midst of these problems at the end of the second year, one of the major owners, Mr. Bianci, contacted a certified management consultant, Bill Walters, Ph.D., CMC. At their initial meeting, Mr. Bianci explained the current situation at the SCS and asked for Dr. Walters' advice. The consultant suggested an organizational assessment consisting of interviews with the three managers, a team-building session using a SWOT Analysis,[1] a separate team-building session with all the SCS store employees, and individual conflict-resolution sessions with the managers. Mr. Bianci agreed with the approach and a consulting contract was executed.

---

[1] *SWOT* is the acronym for a self-analysis technique in which an individual or organization evaluates his or her *strengths, weaknesses,* future *opportunities,* and potential *threats* which might interfere with achieving success. See Appendix 7.

Case Studies

The Consultant's Assessment and Findings on Salmon Creek

Interview and Discussion with SCS Managers as a Group. Dr. Walters scheduled a first meeting with the three managers, Joe, Fred, and Don. The purpose of the session was to examine how the managers as a group felt about the current situation. Not unexpectedly, the managers as a group were cautious in expressing specific (or personal) concerns. During this session, the managers reported general issues that included:

1. *Unclear manager roles and responsibilities.* The managers felt that their responsibilities were ambiguous, poorly defined, and overlapped among the three.
2. *Worker Confusion.* Employees were often confused, due to conflicting instructions from each of the three managers.
3. *Communications problems* existed between the store managers, between managers and employees, and between the tire busters and mechanics.
4. *Hostile workplace environment.* Employees demonstrated an unusually high degree of hostility toward each other and toward the managers.
5. *Poor morale.* Employees exhibited substantial job dissatisfaction and poor morale.
6. *Poor performance* now existed at the SCS, which had not occurred in the past. This included low quality service, scheduling problems, or substandard work.
7. *Changes in scheduling* of individual jobs came from all three managers, with few occurrences when a manager checked with another manager, thus adding to the confusion experienced by the mechanics.
8. *Increased workplace accidents.* A higher than average number of accidents occurred in the store. These included heavy tools or tires dropped on someone's foot, machine breakdowns, and increases in minor injuries.
9. *Customer complaints* increased due to substandard work, such as the wrong tires being installed on vehicles, incorrect air pressure in tires, or lost or misplaced hubcaps.
10. *No information from headquarters* was given to the SCS on any WTA store's performance, company profitability, new developments, or changes. One manager stated, for example, that "We never know how we are doing, or what's going on in the company."

Individual Interviews with the SCS Managers. To gain further information about underlying issues, Dr. Walters held structured interviews and discussions with each of the managers individually. The interview with Joe Martin is described below:

Bill:	Joe, why don't you tell me what's really happening in the store.
Joe:	Well, I'm very frustrated. Everyone has been fighting me ever since I took over two years ago, especially Fred.
Bill:	Why do you think Fred is doing that?
Joe:	He was demoted when I came in. He was store manager for twenty years. When I took over, he became, essentially, the assistant manager. Even though we call him the service manager, and he didn't lose any pay.
Bill:	Wouldn't that make anyone angry? Especially since the owners didn't talk with him before the change took place?
Joe:	Of course! That was poor management by the two owners. On the other hand, that's real life! If Fred couldn't live with that, he should have quit.
Bill:	Fred has been with the company twenty-five years. Twenty years as store manager, right?
Joe:	Sure, but there's more to it than that! The owners were not happy with Fred's management. His profits had been going down while all the other stores were increasing their profits. That's one of the reasons I took over the SCS.
Bill:	Is there some unique legal arrangement for the SCS?
Joe:	Yes, the SCS is incorporated separately as a wholly owned subsidiary of WTA. I am not sure why it was done that way, but the store is still completely controlled by the two majority owners of WTA, Mr. Bianci, and Mr. Steiger.
Bill:	What do you think should be done to resolve the problems at the SCS?
Joe:	One of us has to go!
Bill:	What do you mean?
Joe:	Well, if Fred can't live with the set-up as it is, he should either try to find another assignment in the company or leave WTA. As an owner, I am certainly not going to leave!

Case Studies

Dr. Walters' interview with Fred Denton elicited the following:

Bill: Fred, why don't you tell me what's really going on in the store?

Fred: Well, I'm still very angry about the way I was treated by the owners. I knocked myself out for them for twenty-five years; twenty years as their manager! And then I get kicked in the rear and dumped.

Bill: I understand your feelings! What do you think are the management problems in the store now?

Fred: Joe is a lousy manager. He has no management skills, doesn't know how to relate to people, screws up the scheduling of jobs, annoys people in the shop, and antagonizes customers. He has personal problems.

Bill: What do you mean by *personal problems*?

Fred: He has family problems at home. He has been seeing a psychologist for some time now. He takes several medications and has major mood fluctuations, and he doesn't remember things.

Bill: Doesn't remember things?

Fred: He forgets meetings, forgets the instructions he gives to workers, he can't remember tire orders, or job completion times. Also, he is incapable of enforcing his own decisions.

Bill: Like what?

Fred: Let me give you two examples. He fired Wayne, one of the tire busters, last Tuesday because Wayne was over an hour late reporting to work for four days in a row. When Joe told him he had to go, Wayne started shouting and screaming at him so Joe backed down and let him stay. How's that for managing the work force?

Bill: What's the other example?

Fred: A week ago, I told Joe that one of the manual lifts was broken and had to be replaced. A new lift costs about $200.00. Joe did nothing about it. Yesterday one of the new tire busters tried to use the lift. He didn't know it was broken. The lift gears slipped and it dropped on his foot. I had to take the man to the hospital emergency room. His foot is broke. Now we face a safety inspection and a fine from the state, and probably a lawsuit from the injured man. The whole thing was Joe's fault.

Bill: What do you think should be done to resolve the problems at the SCS?

Fred: One of us has to go! I can't function with Joe any longer. He is creating chaos in the store. Half the tire busters are ready to quit and two of the three mechanics are looking for jobs elsewhere. Also, the store profit has been going downhill since he took over.

Bill: Joe is a part owner. Why should he leave? Would you be willing to quit?

Fred: No way! I invested twenty-five years in the company. If they fire me, I'll hire an attorney and sue them for wrongful discharge. Joe is going to ruin this store! I don't understand why the owners can't see that!

The consultant's meeting with the assistant manager, Don Hagan, revealed that Don had been with SCS for five years before Joe Martin took over. Don confirmed that the store had major problems, which Hagan felt were caused chiefly by the conflict between Joe and Fred. He stated that he himself "tried to stay out" of that conflict. He spent most of his time "managing the mechanics." He felt that "something had to be done about the problem," but also thought that his own position at the SCS would not be substantially affected by any change.

Case Issues/Questions

1. Conduct a case analysis based on the information contained in the case and the information obtained by the consultant:
   a. What are the symptoms?
   b. What are the facts?
   c. What are the causes?

2. Evaluate the approach used by the WTA owners in effecting the change in managers at the SCS two years ago.

3. Develop a procedure for implementing future managerial changes at their stores.

Case Studies

4. What are the alternatives for resolving current problems at the SCS?
   a. What should be done about Joe Martin?
   b. What should be done about Fred Denton?
   c. What are the potential implications for the company if either Joe or Fred are terminated? If both are terminated?
   d. What should be done about the employees' low morale, job dissatisfaction, and related personnel problems at the SCS?

5. What are your recommendations to Mr. Bianci and Mr. Steiger for resolving the current problems at the SCS?
   a. Prepare specific solutions including, as appropriate, organization charts, implementation timetables, and personnel actions.
   b. Include justifications for your recommendations: Why they are preferable to other alternatives; what legal, performance, cost/benefit, strategy implications need to be considered, etc.

6. Evaluate and develop your prediction of the most likely future of the SCS if the owners do not accept and implement your recommendations. Outline specific outcomes, implications, probabilities, and risk factors.

Western Tire and Alignment, Inc.
Part B

Introduction. See Part A for history and description of WTA. Note especially the Salmon Creek Store (SCS).

The Case. As part of the organizational consultation, Dr. Walters conducted a team-building session with all employees of the SCS held on store premises after business hours on a Thursday evening. The SCS employed three mechanics and twelve tire busters, all of whom participated in this session. The three managers were also present. Participants sat in a semi-circle arrangement as requested by the consultant.

The session began with the use of an abbreviated SWOT Analysis: Using a "round-robin" approach, each participant was asked to identify the store's weaknesses. Responses were written on flipchart-size blank paper that was taped onto the walls. This process was continued until no further comments were offered. The managers' participation was noteworthy: Fred (service manager), and Don (assistant manager) both joined in. The owner-manager, Joe, sat silently throughout and did not offer any input or comments.

Results of Abbreviated SWOT Analysis. This SWOT Analysis elicited numerous responses from participants. These responses were later grouped into three major categories:

A. *Store/physical problems.*

1. We need to do something about our WTA sign. People cannot see it from the street.
2. We don't have enough space to maximize productivity.
3. Scheduling is confusing and inconsistent. It causes frustration and conflict. It affects customer service.
4. Phone and radio calls are not answered promptly.
5. We don't have enough tire busters.
6. We need another service truck driver.
7. A truck should replace the service trailer.
8. Our ad in the phone book is out of date.

B. *Interpersonal problems (employees-management, and employee-employee).*

1. We get no recognition from upper management when we do a good job, when someone has twenty years of service, or if someone is recovering from an injury.
2. We have poor communication with our managers and between ourselves. There is no teamwork. There is poor delegation of responsibilities.
3. We don't have a good system for discussing our problems with managers and with each other.
4. There is too much horseplay and objectionable language. Customers can hear it in the waiting area.

C. *Company procedures, policies, and problems.*

1. The organization in different stores is not uniform: Each store operates by itself. In some stores people are paid more for the same job/work done in other stores.
2. We don't have a training program for new hires and for current employees to advance into higher positions.
3. Our pay scales are below average for the Salmon Creek area. This is particularly true for mechanics' salaries.
4. We should have job descriptions, written pay scales, and promotion policies.

Case Issues/Questions

1. Prepare an analysis of the SWOT results.
2. Prepare a set of recommendations to management, based on your analysis of the SWOT exercise. Consider as part of your evaluation and recommendations the following findings:
   a. Key problems articulated by the group.
   b. Apparent focus of conflict.
   c. Personnel issues related to administration, training, compensation, etc.
   d. Apparent communication problems between managers, between employees, and between headquarters (i.e., owners) and the SCS.
   e. Work processes: scheduling, staffing, planning, etc.
   f. Potential legal problems related to all the above.

APPENDICES

Appendix 1
Sexual Harassment Policy Statement
Department of Fair Employment and Housing
State of California DFEH-185 (12/92)

Preventing Sexual Harassment

A program to eliminate sexual harassment from the workplace is not only required by law, but it is the most practical way to avoid or limit damages if harassment should occur despite preventive efforts.

Complaint Procedure

An employer should take immediate and appropriate action when he or she knows, or should have known, that sexual harassment has occurred. An employer must take effective action to stop any further harassment and to ameliorate any effects of the harassment. To those ends, the employer's policy should include provisions to:

- Fully inform complainant of his or her rights and any obligations to secure those rights.
- Fully and effectively investigate. It must be immediate, thorough, objective and complete. All those with information on the matter should be interviewed. Determinations must be made and the results communicated to the complainant, to the alleged harasser, and, as appropriate, to all others directly concerned.
- If proven, there must be prompt and effective remedial action. First, appropriate action must be taken against the harasser and communicated to the complainant. Second, steps must be taken to prevent any further harassment. Third, appropriate action must be taken to remedy the complainant's loss, if any.

Training of All Individuals in The Workplace

All employees must receive from their employers a copy of this pamphlet (DFEH-185) or an equivalent document. Supervisory personnel should be educated about their specific responsibilities. Rank and file employees should be cautioned against using peer pressure to discourage harassment victims from using the internal grievance procedure.

Appendix 2
Sexual Harassment Prevention Checklist

1. Notify your employees with a written, posted policy statement that sexual harassment is illegal and will not be tolerated.

2. Establish or make sure that all employees are aware of the complaint procedure for dealing with problems they encounter.

3. Designate one person in your organization (by name and phone number) responsible for working with persons who are believed to have been sexually harassed.

4. Talk with subordinates about sexual harassment problems in a clear, direct, and serious manner. Answer their questions and spell out what is expected of them.

5. Inform your employees that sexual harassment will be treated as serious, illegal employee misconduct, and that harassers will be dealt with firmly.

6. Establish clear lines of communication with subordinates; make it known that you have an open door policy to discuss problems with sexual harassment.

7. Be alert to what is happening between and among employees; try to anticipate problems and "nip them in the bud."

8. Include sexual harassment awareness as part of the orientation and training of new employees.

9. Deal with sexual harassment problems promptly; help prevent future occurrences.

Appendix 3
Sample Interview Items

1. Discuss confidentiality and privacy of interviews; how the interview material will be used.

2. Establish employee's characteristics:
    - employee's age, sex, and manner of presentation.
    - position or status in the department
    - job tasks
    - length of time with the company; within the department

3. Briefly discuss findings of the organizational survey with employee.

4. Determine:
    - what the employee is most satisfied with in the department
    - what frustrates the employee the most
    - what the employee thinks ought to be done to improve the department

5. Determine interpersonal aspects:
    - the nature of the employee's relationship with co-workers. If applicable: what ways the employee thinks those relationships can be improved
    - the nature of the employee's relationship with his or her supervisor. If applicable: what ways employee thinks the relationship can be improved

6. Wrap-up:
    - summarize the session with the employee
    - clarify any issues that emerged during the interview
    - reinforce again the confidential nature of the interview
    - indicate your availability for future private discussion, if appropriate

Appendix 4
Sample Brief: Executive Summary

Organizational Assessment — Executive Summary
Rogers and Associates

- **Organizational assessment procedures**:
  1. Most employees (98 %) completed organizational survey.
  2. Managers and all subordinates completed leadership survey.
  3. Selected personnel were interviewed (five managers, ten subordinates).

- **Assessment findings :**
  1. Employees consistently rated the leadership, job structure, and performance and development systems below-average.
  2. Subordinates consistently rated their managers below-average in leadership.
  3. All managers rated themselves above-average in leadership.
  4. Interviewees felt that S. Donnelley was not as good a manager as the retired one; that the department's service to the company had deteriorated under her management.

- **Recommendations :**
  1. Add a deputy manager to the department.
  2. Offer training to all managers in leadership and interpersonal, diversity, and communications skills development.
  3. Implement team-building in Susan Donnelley's department.

Appendix 5
Sample Contents of Written Primary Report

		page
	Introduction	iv
I.	The Executive Summary	1
II.	The Primary Report	18
	Introduction	18
	The Organizational Assessment Survey	18
	The Learning Organization Practices Profile (LOPP)	19
	Characteristics of a "Learning Organization"	22
	LOPP Data Analysis and Results	26
	The Managers' Survey	29
	The Leadership Profile Inventory (LPI)	29
	Characteristics of "Leadership"	30
	LPI Data Analysis and Results	32
	The Structured Interviews	34
	Definition of *Structured Interviews*	35
	Content Analysis of Interviews and Results	36
III.	Team-Building	
	Definition of *Focused Team-Building*	38
	Team-Building Results	39
	Branch Team-Building	39
	Managers' Team-Building	40
	Quality Assurance Team-Building	41
IV.	Summary	42
V.	References	43
VI.	Appendices	44
VII.	Alphabetical Index	57

Appendix 6
Code of Ethics of the Institute of Management Consultants

Clients
1. We will serve our clients with integrity, competence, and objectivity.
2. We will keep client information and records of client engagements confidential and will use proprietary client information only with the client's permission.
3. We will not take advantage of confidential client information for ourselves or our firms.
4. We will not allow conflicts of interest which [sic] provide a competitive advantage to one client through our use of confidential information from another client who is a direct competitor without that competitor's permission.

Engagements
5. We will accept only engagements for which we are qualified by our experience and competence.
6. We will assign staff to client engagements in accordance with their experience, knowledge, and expertise.
7. We will immediately acknowledge any influences on our objectivity to our clients, and will offer to withdraw from a consulting engagement when our objectivity or integrity might be impaired.

Fees
8. We will agree independently and in advance on the basis for our fees and expenses, and will charge fees and expenses that are reasonable, legitimate, and commensurate with the services we deliver and the responsibility we accept.
9. We will disclose to our clients in advance any fees or commissions that we will receive for equipment, supplies, or services we recommend to our clients.

Profession
10. We will respect the intellectual property rights of our clients, other consulting firms, and sole practitioners, and will not use proprietary information or methodologies without permission.
11. We will not advertise our services in a deceptive manner and will not misrepresent the consulting profession, consulting firms, or sole practitioners.
12. We will report violations of this Code of Ethics.

Reprinted with the permission of the Institute of Management Consultants

Appendix 7
The SWOT Analysis

Purposes:
- To help individuals or organizations identify their strengths and weaknesses in relation to achieving goals, opportunities toward realizing goals, and threats that thwart or impede achievement of goals.
- To help clients define their attributes and circumstances realistically.

Settings:
Administered and discussed with an individual, or administered and discussed with a group.

Materials:
Paper and pen, or flipchart and markers.

Procedures:
Generate attributes. Say to an individual or group: "Please list or identify at least three strengths (**S**) that will help you achieve your goal. We will discuss them after you have identified weaknesses, opportunities, and threats." The items are written down by the individual, or written on a flipchart in a group setting. Do the same in turn for **W**-weaknesses, **O**-opportunities, and **T**-threats.

Discuss each attribute in turn with the client(s). Discourage them from making value judgments about any attribute. Objectives of discussion are to demonstrate to clients how they *think* about themselves and their circumstances and how realistic their perceptions are.

Re-write **S, W, O,** and **T** items after reality-testing discussion.

Options/Comments:
- While performing all steps is the most productive method, the interviewer and respondent might wish to perform an abbreviated version, depending on situational needs.
- Written materials belong to the respondent. For research purposes, assure the respondent of the interviewer's clear understanding of confidentiality and have the respondent sign a release of information so that the interviewer can keep the materials for scientific purposes.

References

Bennis, W. and Mische, M., *The 21st Century Organization.* San Diego, CA: Pfeifferand Co., 1995.

Byars, L. and Rue, L., *Human Resource Management.* Chicago, IL: Irwin, 1997.

Carnall, C., *Managing Change in Organizations.* Englewood Cliffs, NJ: Prentice-Hall, 1995.

David, F., *Strategic Management.* Englewood Cliffs, NJ: Prentice-Hall, 1997.

Deming, W. Edwards, *Out of the Crisis.* Cambridge, MA: Massachusetts Institute of Technology, 1986.

Fernandez, J., *Managing a Diverse Workforce.* Lexington, MA: Lexington Books, 1991.

Hammer, M. and Champy, J., *Reengineering the Corporation.* New York, NY: Harper Collins, 1993.

Hodgetts, R. and Luthans, F., *International Management.* New York, NY: McGraw-Hill, 1994.

Jamieson, D. and O' Mara, J., *Managing Workforce 2000.* San Francisco, CA: Jossey-Bass, 1991.

Kouzes, J. M. and Posner, B.Z., *The Leadership Challenge: How to Get Extraordinary Things Done in Organizations.* San Francisco, CA: Jossey-Bass, 1987.

Kouzes, J.M. and Posner, B.Z., *The Leadership Practices Inventory (LPI).* San Diego, CA: Pfeiffer and Co., 1993.

Litterer, Joseph A., *The Analysis of Organizations.* New York, NY: John Wiley and Sons, Inc., 1965.

O'Brien, M. J., *The Learning Organization Practices Profile (LOPP).* San Diego, CA: Pfeiffer and Co., 1994.

O'Brien, M. J., *The Learning Organization Practices Profile: Guide to Administration and Implementation.* San Diego, CA: Pfeiffer and Co., 1994.

Petrocelli, E. and Repa, B.K., *Sexual Harassment on the Job.* Berkeley, CA: Nolo Press, 1997.

Rogers, R. E., *Corporate Strategy and Planning.* New York, NY: Grid/Wiley, 1981.

Rogers, R. E., *Implementation of Total Quality Management.* New York: Haworth Press, 1996.

Rogers, R. E. and McIntire, R., *Organization and Management Theory.* New York, NY: John Wiley and Sons, 1983.

Robbins, S., *Organizational Behavior.* Englewood Cliffs, NJ: Prentice-Hall, 1998.

Weelins, R., Byham, W., and Dixon, G., *Inside Teams.* San Francisco, CA: Jossey-Bass, 1994.